THE HISTORY OF BRONZE AND IRON AGE ISRAEL

ESSENTIALS OF BIBLICAL STUDIES

Series Editor

Patricia K. Tull, Louisville Presbyterian Theological Seminary

Reading Hebrew Bible Narratives
J. Andrew Dearman

The History of Bronze and Iron Age Israel
Victor H. Matthews

New Testament Christianity in the Roman World
Harry O. Maier

Women in the New Testament World
Susan E. Hylen

The History of Bronze and Iron Age Israel

VICTOR H. MATTHEWS

Oxford University Press is a department of the University of Oxford. It furthers the University's objective of excellence in research, scholarship, and education by publishing worldwide. Oxford is a registered trade mark of Oxford University Press in the UK and certain other countries.

Published in the United States of America by Oxford University Press
198 Madison Avenue, New York, NY 10016, United States of America.

Library of Congress Cataloging-in-Publication Data
Names: Matthews, Victor Harold, author
Title: The history of Bronze and Iron Age Israel / by Victor H. Matthews.
Description: New York, NY : Oxford University Press, [2019] |
Includes bibliographical references and index.
Identifiers: LCCN 2018013399 (print) | LCCN 2018015025 (ebook) |
ISBN 9780190231163 (updf) | ISBN 9780190231170 (epub) |
ISBN 9780190231149 (hardcover) | ISBN 9780190231156 (paperback) |
ISBN 9780190231187 (online content)
Subjects: LCSH: Jews—History—To 586 B.C. | Bronze age—Palestine. |
Iron age—Palestine. | Bible. Old Testament—History of Biblical events. |
Palestine—History—To 70 A.D.
Classification: LCC DS121 (ebook) | LCC DS121 .M382944 2019 (print) |
DDC 933—dc23
LC record available at https://lccn.loc.gov/2018013399

CONTENTS

SERIES INTRODUCTION

The past three decades have seen an explosion of approaches to study of the Bible, as older exegetical methods have been joined by a variety of literary, anthropological, and social models. Interfaith collaboration has helped change the field, and the advent of more cultural diversity among biblical scholars in the west and around the world has broadened our reading and interpretation of the Bible. These changes have also fueled interest in Scripture's past: both the ancient Near Eastern and Mediterranean worlds out of which Scripture came and the millennia of premodern interpretation through which it traveled to our day. The explosion of information and perspectives is so vast that no one textbook can any longer address the many needs of seminaries and colleges where the Bible is studied.

In addition to these developments in the field itself are changes in the students. Traditionally the domain of seminaries, graduate schools, and college and university religion classes, now biblical study also takes place in a host of alternative venues. As lay leadership in local churches develops, non-traditional, weekend, and online preparatory classes have mushroomed. As seminaries in Africa, Asia, and Latin America grow, particular need for inexpensive, easily available materials is clear. As religious controversies over the Bible's origins and norms continue to dominate the airwaves, congregation members and even curious non-religious folk seek reliable paths into particular topics. And teachers themselves continue to seek guidance in areas of the ever-expanding field of scriptural study with which they may be less than familiar.

A third wave of changes also makes this series timely: shifts in the publishing industry itself. Technologies and knowledge are shifting so rapidly that large books are out of date almost before they are in print. The internet and the growing popularity of e-books call for flexibility and accessibility in marketing and sales. If the days when one expert can sum up the field in a textbook are gone, also gone are the days when large, expensive multi-authored tomes are attractive to students, teachers, and other readers.

During my own years of seminary teaching, I have tried to find just the right book or books for just the right price, at just the right reading level for my students, with just enough information to orient them without drowning them in excess reading. For all the reasons stated above, this search was all too often less than successful. So I was excited to be asked to help Oxford University Press assemble a select crew of leading scholars to create a series that would respond to such classroom challenges. Essentials of Biblical Studies comprises freestanding, relatively brief, accessibly written books that provide orientation to the Bible's contents, its ancient contexts, its interpretive methods and history, and its themes and figures. Rather than a one-size-had-better-fit-all approach, these books may be mixed and matched to suit the objectives of a variety of classroom venues as well as the needs of individuals wishing to find their way into unfamiliar topics.

I am confident that our book authors will join me in returning enthusiastic thanks to the editorial staff at Oxford University Press for their support and guidance, especially Theo Calderara, who shepherded the project in its early days, and Dr. Steve Wiggins, who has been a most wise and steady partner in this work since joining OUP in 2013.

Patricia K. Tull
Series Editor

THE HISTORY OF BRONZE AND IRON AGE ISRAEL

1

Placing Ancient Israel in Its Ancient Near Eastern Context

A NUMBER OF TOPICS ARE explored in this opening chapter. The chapter begins with a brief discussion of the methods that will be employed in examining the history writing (historiography) of the biblical writers and editors, and also of the task associated with writing a history of ancient Israel. That discussion will also include the current library of extrabiblical sources that is available to scholars. Having established a methodological tone, attention will then be given to the role of historical geography as it relates to a study of the history of the countries of the Levant. Each region will be examined separately along with the cultures that developed there. Finally, an introduction to the values and limitations of archaeology will be sketched out, with a focus on their use in reconstructing everyday life in antiquity. Naturally, each of these topics is also explored in more depth in later chapters. However, for the sake of continuity they are introduced here so that readers will have a preliminary familiarity before they are drawn into the events from each period of ancient Israel's story.

METHODS IN THE RECONSTRUCTION OF ANCIENT ISRAEL'S HISTORY

Historians should carefully make use of all available data. In the case of ancient Israel, that includes extrabiblical texts, manuscripts of the biblical texts, and current archaeological data. Historians should also use methods for historical research and social scientific examination of cultures that have been developed over the past century. That is not to say that all historians agree on either the relevance or reliability of our current data on ancient Israel or of the methods to employ. In this section, the controversies and current trends in reconstructing the past will be discussed.

Because of its association with three major faith communities (Jewish, Christian, and Muslim), the Bible is often at the center of the debate over ancient Israel. Those who rely on a faith commitment to guide their interpretation of the biblical materials and see the biblical account as a fully accurate account of Israel's history are referred to today as "maximalists."[1] Other scholars, who take the view that the Bible is basically a fictionalized account of events created in the Hellenistic period (third to second centuries BCE) by scribes and priests, who wished to create a foundation story for their community, are referred to as "minimalists."[2] Neither of these polar opposites is willing to modify their respective position to take into account physical or textual data that modify or negate their fundamental conclusions. For the maximalists, that would require them to accept the view that the biblical materials are not the inerrant word of God and that the purpose of archaeology and textual studies is not to prove the veracity of the Bible's account. For the minimalists, that would require a fuller acceptance of the value of archaeological findings and the authenticity of ancient documents that indicate that the nations of Israel and Judah had a historical existence prior to the eighth century BCE. They would have to acknowledge that pure objectivity is not really possible and that it must be balanced by reasoned speculation.[3]

The debate between these two positions occupied a great deal of energy and produced a significant level of rancor within the scholarly community over the past twenty-five years.[4] While many felt that the minimalists were asking good questions and that it was important to analyze the evidence very carefully, it was felt that the sometimes strained efforts on their part to dismiss portions of that data simply went too far. Many scholars also felt that the position of the maximalists was too restrictive and kept archaeologists, philologists, and historians from following the interpretive path that newly discovered evidence provided.

It is a middle ground that now attracts the efforts of many scholars today. They can recognize that the biblical materials are a valuable source of information if examined critically and with the understanding that these documents developed over the centuries into the canonical texts we now possess. It is also possible to describe the biblical writers and editors as history writers, at least to the extent that what they produced is based on their compilation and evaluation of available sources. Of course, they, like all historians, had their own agendas and made judgments about what would be included in the text based on theological, political, or cultural preconceptions.[5]

Today textual comparisons begin with the received Hebrew Masoretic text (dating to c. 500 CE) and includes the third-century BCE Greek translation of the Hebrew Scriptures (the Septuagint), as well as the materials contained in the Dead Sea scrolls (c. 100 BCE to 70 CE) and other ancient manuscripts that contain portions of the biblical text. These materials play an important role in the process of reconstructing the canonical process and determining the best reading of the text.

The use of extrabiblical documents began during the nineteenth century CE when a great furor arose over the decipherment of Egyptian hieroglyphic texts and the discovery of thousands of Mesopotamian cuneiform inscriptions and clay tablets. After these works were deciphered, scholars and the general public had access to the literary heritage of the ancient Near East. That in turn led to a more critical examination and interpretation of the biblical text. While there is no firm consensus among scholars on exactly how or when the biblical materials were edited and shaped by events and the development of theological positions, it is assumed today that this editing process did occur. Some point to various strains of editing that led to the collection of materials, such as the stories in Judges or the annals of the kings of Israel and Judah. They posit the existence of master scribal/priestly scholars that some call the Deuteronomistic Historian, who at the end of the monarchy period in the sixth century BCE compiled available source material into the text found in Joshua through 2 Kings.

Scholars also describe an exilic or postexilic priestly editor, who shaped those portions of the biblical text that dealt with the activities of the priestly community, the sacrificial rituals, and the concept of ritual purity for a people chosen by God. Despite the efforts of scholars over many years, what exactly occurred is unknown and therefore is still to be found in the realm of educated speculation. But speculation and raising questions are the stock-in-trade for historians. When a paradigm of understanding stifles critical examination of the origins of ancient Israel, new understanding and progress are stopped.

Given that reality, what can be said about the biblical materials as one source of data for the reconstruction of the history of ancient Israel? First, the Bible was not composed in a cultural vacuum and it did not emerge full-blown from the imagination of a group of scribes. Rather than a piece of fiction or a theological treatise designed solely to justify the needs of a postexilic or Hellenistic Jewish community, it contains references both to actual historical events as well as to foundation stories that serve as etiological explanations for their concept of a covenantal relationship with their God. As a result, it is possible to write a history that is based on "well-argued plausibilities" that represent a possible past and is subject to future testing and examination while serving to challenge other possible pasts, thus providing a logical reconstruction.[6]

To be sure, the exilic experience starting in 597 BCE brought the people of Judah into close contact with the Mesopotamian cultural world, and that contributed to the editing of ancient Israel's foundation stories. The etiological accounts in Genesis, for instance, clearly have Mesopotamian roots traceable to the Babylonian *Enuma Elish* creation story and the flood story in the Gilgamesh epic. The legal materials in Exodus through Deuteronomy did benefit in their formulation from the long heritage of Mesopotamian legal tradition, including Hammurabi's Code (eighteenth century BCE). Wisdom literature, especially the book of Proverbs, draws on the rich Egyptian wisdom tradition contained in the Teachings of Ptah-Hotep, the Teachings of Amen-em-ope, and others. Even the prophetic materials have clear ties to the extensive prophetic and omen literature of Mesopotamia's various cultures. However, it is unlikely that Israel's first contact with this cultural heritage came only during and after the exile. There are simply too many parallels in the language of the biblical writers and prophets with eighth- and seventh-century BCE Assyrian texts to suggest that Israel's scribal community was not well schooled in the style of their political masters prior to the exile.[7]

Extrabiblical Sources

In subsequent chapters in this volume, each of the time periods associated with the ancient Israelites is examined. During some of these periods, there is very little in the way of verifiable data upon which to reconstruct a history. As we move down the timeline from the Middle Bronze IIB-C (c. 1800–1570 BCE) to the Late Bronze Age (c. 1570–1200 BCE) and into the Iron I-A (c. 1200–1140 BCE), a picture begins to emerge based on a few extrabiblical inscriptions and a body of archaeological data. However, it will only be during the Iron II period (c. 1140–701 BCE) that the level of information rises to a point where it is possible to say that a people identifying themselves as the nations of Israel and Judah occupied a number of sites throughout Canaan and had interaction with the major super powers of the day.

Table 1.1 lists the major extrabiblical inscriptions that are relevant to the history of ancient Israel. They are discussed in subsequent chapters within the context of the time periods to which they belong. Note that there are a number of literary parallels between ancient Near Eastern texts and the biblical narrative, but they will be discussed separately since their relevance to historical reconstruction has more to do with cultural and social development than as indicators of specific historical events.[8]

THE ROLE OF GEOGRAPHY

Throughout this volume there are constant references to peoples and places (regions and cities) and topographical features. It is therefore necessary for any student of history to be able to visualize the physical environment that cradled the civilization under discussion. River systems, mountains, valleys, deserts, deposits of minerals (salt) and metals (copper, iron, gold), caves, and springs all play their part in the events of history. Each of the major regions and civilizations of the ancient Near East is discussed here with attention given to the essentials of

Table 1.1

MAJOR EXTRA-BIBLICAL DOCUMENTS RELEVANT TO THE HISTORY OF ANCIENT ISRAEL

National Origin and Date	*Inscription Title*	*Relevance*
Egypt—fifteenth century BCE	Annals of Tuthmosis III	Egyptian expansion into Canaan
Egypt—fourteenth century BCE	El Amarna texts	Demonstrates growing unrest in Canaan—*habiru* banditry
Egypt—1208 BCE	Merneptah Stele	First mention of people named Israel outside the Bible
Egypt—1186 BCE	Annals of Ramesses III	Reports of conflict with the Sea Peoples
Egypt—c. 925 BCE	Shoshenq I Bubastite Portal	Possible parallel with Shishak in 1 Kgs 14 in dispute
Moab—c. 835 BCE	Annals of Mesha	Parallels 2 Kgs 3 and Israel's invasion of Moab
Assyria—853 BCE	Annals of Shalmaneser III—Kurkh Monolith	Coalition of small states opposes Assyria—includes Ahab among the allies
Assyria—845 BCE	Annals of Shalmaneser III—Black Obelisk	Defeat of Hazael of Aram; depiction of Jehu of Israel paying tribute
Israel—798 BCE	Tel Dan Inscription	Mention of "House of David" in Syrian victory stele; parallel to 2 Kgs 9:1–10:28

(continued)

Table 1.1

CONTINUED

National Origin and Date	*Inscription Title*	*Relevance*
Assyria—722–721 BCE	Annals of Sargon II	Destruction of Samaria and deportation of Israel's people
Assyria—701 BCE	Annals of Sennacherib	Siege of Jerusalem / Hezekiah's ransom payment
Babylon—598 BCE	Babylonian Chronicle	Nebuchadnezzar II captures Jerusalem; deports Jehoiachin
Judah—587–586 BCE	Lachish Letters	Ostraca describing last days of Judah before Babylonian conquest

their historical geography and their interaction with the other major cultures that developed in the Levant. In this way it is possible to provide a framework for their cultural development and explain how and why they came to be important to the history of ancient Israel.

That is why it is only possible to write a history of the ancient Israelites if they are considered within their spatial context. Attention must be given not only to major events and to the players (peoples and their principal rulers), but also to the places they inhabit. An essential element of that task is to describe their physical environment, including the basic features of topography, natural resources, and climate, since these will be determining factors in how their society is shaped, the ability of their economy to expand, and the extent to which they will be influenced by other cultures.

It is an interesting reality that so much history has been focused on a very small region of the earth. To be sure, the earliest high civilizations appeared in the Nile River Valley of Egypt and between the Tigris and Euphrates rivers in Mesopotamia. But when these ancient giants began to look beyond their borders, they discovered that they were separated by the land bridge of Syria-Palestine. As a result, this region throughout its history has functioned as a highway, a trade route, a buffer zone, and a battleground. Therefore, to escape the trap of focusing exclusively on ancient Israelite culture in a social vacuum during the second and first millennia BCE, it becomes necessary to focus our attention, as the ancient rulers of the Near East did, and see Syria-Palestine as key for international politics and trade. The history of the dominant cultures of Egypt, Asia Minor (modern Turkey), and Mesopotamia and their social, economic, and political ambitions to control Syria-Palestine will dominate ancient Israel's development and our discussion.

Egypt

To discuss the history of Egypt without explaining the overriding influence of the annual south to north inundation of the Nile River is unthinkable. It created both a spatial orientation and a watery highway for the region from Upper Egypt in the south to Lower Egypt and the delta in the north. The very constancy of this annual event allowed the Egyptians to harness the Nile's potential and develop an extensive system of irrigation canals and sluice gates that managed the flow of water to their fields and deposited the rich silt that promoted their harvests and turned Egypt into the bread basket of the ancient world. Egyptian religion attributed this phenomenon to divine benevolence and gave their people a belief in a well-regulated existence. It is not surprising that the pharaohs took advantage of the systematic renewal of the nation's agricultural resources by creating an ideology of divine rule that placed them within the pantheon of the gods and thus responsible for the well-being of the people.

Rulership of Egypt was centered in several important cities and shifted from the northern capital at Memphis to the southern capital at Thebes over the course of its history. While Egyptian culture has produced spectacular examples of monumental construction (pyramids, palaces, and temples), these works are more a reflection of the divine persona of the pharaohs and the power of the priests, who were associated with their major gods (including Amun Re, Osiris, Isis, Horus, and Thoth). Despite the great emphasis on agricultural activity, Egyptian texts describe a wide range of professions, including skilled artisans and artists, builders and architects, and soldiers and scribes. Since Egyptian hieroglyphic writing is extremely complex (based on a syllabic rather than an alphabetic system), professional scribes became a powerful group in society, filling the bureaucratic offices that managed all aspects of the economy and the distribution of goods and services throughout the nation.

Once the regions of Upper and Lower Egypt were united under the 1st Dynasty of pharaohs (c. 3150–c. 2890 BCE), the nation was able to develop independently and without significant interference from other cultures because of the natural boundaries that guarded Egypt's heartland from invaders. Egypt's western borders were protected by an extensive desert region that dominated much of North Africa. The cataracts along the Nile south of Thebes prevented easy navigation of the river or invasion by peoples from the south. The Red Sea provided a sea link to the trade goods and spices of the Arabian Peninsula and India, and it guarded Egypt's eastern coastline. With only a very narrow strip of land tying Egypt to the Sinai Peninsula on its eastern border, it was possible to militarize that approach and place a series of fortresses along it to control the trade routes. Finally, the waters of the Mediterranean Sea served both as a maritime link to the cultures of Minoan Crete and Mycenaean Greece to the north and as a barrier to raiders.

Of course, Egypt was not invulnerable to invasion or cultural decline. Its history is marked by periodic breakdowns when the leadership of a ruling dynasty faltered and the economy suffered. These Intermediate Periods (2181–2040 BCE and c. 1782–c. 1570 BCE) divide the Old Kingdom from the Middle and New Kingdoms in Egyptian history. They were characterized by social upheaval and insecurity that made the land vulnerable to internal political decay and intrusion by outside invaders. For example, foreigners collectively referred to by the Egyptians as the Hyksos conquered Lower Egypt in the seventeenth century BCE during the Second Intermediate Period. They ruled that portion of the country from their capital at Avaris in the Nile Delta for over a hundred years (c. 1630–1523 BCE) before being expelled by a native Egyptian dynasty that established the New Kingdom. In fact, it was the period of Hyksos rule that drew Egypt's attention more fully to Canaan.

Between approximately 1500 and 1150 BCE, Egypt invested a great deal of effort in extending its political and economic hegemony into the eastern border area. Although Egypt had no policy on colonizing Syria-Palestine, the pharaohs maintained their control over the region through a series of political appointments and client rulers. Regular reports from these officials, based in Gezer, Lachish, Byblos, Megiddo, and Shechem, kept their king apprised of their success in exploiting Canaan's natural resources and the problems that they and Egyptian merchants occasionally faced from brigands and rebels. The El Amarna tablets that date to the fourteenth century contain examples of these reports and an account of growing unrest in the area during a period when Egypt's ruler, the pharaoh Akhenaten (1353–1335 BCE), was focused more on his religious reform in Egypt than on his political and economic interests in Syria-Palestine.

Despite this lag in effective leadership, Egypt certainly viewed Syria-Palestine as a strategic area and that brought the pharaohs of the 18th Dynasty to once again expand fuller control over the region in the thirteenth century BCE. It also brought them into conflict with the Hittite empire in Asia Minor (modern-day Turkey), which had begun extending its hegemony south into Syria-Palestine during the fourteenth century BCE. Ultimately, after exhausting themselves in their military rivalry with the Hittites, it would be another group of invaders, known as the Sea Peoples, that cost Egypt its control over Syria-Palestine. That in turn set the stage for the reshuffling of the cultural composition of Syria-Palestine in the period after 1200 BCE. Over the next six hundred years, Egypt continued to conduct periodic military or diplomatic intrusions into Syria-Palestine's territory and history, but it never again had a free hand in exploiting the area's resources or peoples. Instead various Mesopotamian empires (Assyrian and Babylonian) were the prime movers in manipulating Syria-Palestine and its people to their advantage during the period between 900 and 586 BCE.

Mesopotamia

Civilization begins in Mesopotamia (modern-day Iraq) in the marshes of the southern reaches of the delta, created by the draining of the Tigris and Euphrates rivers into the Persian Gulf. In this area known as Sumer, a number of cultural and technological developments took place between 3500 and 2500 BCE. These included the invention of massive irrigation systems to water fields away from the rivers and the development of strong centralized states to manage the increasingly complex infrastructure needs of a growing population. During this time, several major city-states emerged at Ur, Kish, Uruk, and Nippur and they competed for dominance. Over the next millennia, Mesopotamian culture expanded northward, up the twin river system with new capitals (Babylon and Nineveh) becoming the center of culture, commerce, and political power.

As in Egypt, monumental construction served as a form of political propaganda that exalted the power of kings and provided a physical platform for a powerful priestly community, who managed the ritual performances associated with the worship of their many gods (Marduk, Enki/Ea, Enlil, Ashur, and Ishtar/Inanna among others). However, these monarchs, while acknowledging that kingship had "come down from heaven" and been given into their hands,[9] never identified themselves as divine. As was the case in Egypt, a powerful scribal community emerged to produce the Mesopotamian cuneiform records of business transactions, government communications and reports, legal texts, and a growing body of epic and wisdom literature.

Where Egypt and Mesopotamia markedly differed was in their regional topography. Egypt was basically a closed system centered on the Nile and surrounded by natural barriers. Mesopotamia was located in a huge flood plain. Archaeological excavations have uncovered destruction layers and huge deposits of silt that indicate the entire region was subject to periodic and massive floods. The annual levels were based on the amount of snowmelt in the mountains of eastern Asia Minor rather than rainfall. Mesopotamia also lacks the physical barriers that benefited Egyptian civilization. The region was open to invaders from all directions. As a result, the history of that region was characterized by the rise and fall of civilizations as they faced pressure from migrating populations or armed invasion. Interestingly, each successive culture adapted aspects of the previous one, such as the use of cuneiform, as it came to power.

The Sumerian city-states eventually fell victim to the emergence of the Akkadian rulers, starting with Sargon I (c. 2334–2279 BCE). Similarly, the Amorite kings of Babylon, including Hammurabi (1792–1750 BCE), took their turn dominating affairs and combining the many small states into an empire. Finally, after a period of several centuries when Mesopotamia was divided into small kingdoms, the Neo-Assyrians from their northern territories on the Tigris River gained dominance over all of Mesopotamia after c. 900 BCE. Their imperial ambitions ultimately extended their rule westward to encompass all of Syria-Palestine. Their success in expanding their empire brought them into direct conflict with Egypt. The super-power struggle between them reduced Israel and Judah to the status of Assyrian client states before the northern kingdom of Israel was destroyed in 721 BCE by Sargon II and its people scattered throughout Assyria's vast expanse of territories.

Mesopotamia bred one final empire that had a devastating impact on the remaining kingdom of Judah. The Chaldeans or Neo-Babylonians, under the leadership of Nebuchadnezzar II (605–562 BCE), brought a violent end to the crumbling Assyrian empire at the Battle of Carchemish in 605 BCE. Very quickly they swept aside the Egyptians, who had gained temporary control of Syria-Palestine and attempted to manage the area with a series of native puppet rulers. That proved unsatisfactory and after quelling repeated revolts, the Neo-Babylonians utterly destroyed Jerusalem in 587 BCE, took a large portion of the population into exile in Mesopotamia, and ended the Judean monarchy that had extended back to King David (2 Kgs 25:1–21).

It is important to note that these successive Mesopotamian empires and their ambitions to dominate the areas to their west and ultimately to control the commercially oriented cities of the Mediterranean coast of Syria and Phoenicia also have a topographical origin. Mesopotamia, except for its river-based link into the Persian Gulf, is landlocked. In order to engage in trade except along the Tigris and Euphrates rivers, it was necessary to travel by caravan routes overland south into Arabia, north into Asia Minor, west to the Mediterranean coast, and down into Syria-Palestine. There are many examples in the records of Mesopotamian kings of their annual expeditions to "reach the sea" or to exploit the cedar forests of Lebanon. In an age before highways and motorized travel, expansion meant the extension of political hegemony and supply lines over the lands of the peoples along the major trade routes. And, since these people always took advantage of every apparent weakness of the empire to rebel, regular military expeditions were required to quell rebellions and refresh treaty agreements. As a result, the ideology of kingship was based around three principles: (1) public devotion to their patron god, (2) construction or renovation of monumental architecture, and (3) regular military campaigns.

Syria-Palestine

The physical reality for Syria-Palestine and the trigger for much of its history is that it lay between two major civilizations. With the deserts of Arabia and southern Syria forming a barrier to direct travel from the heart of Mesopotamia to the west, it was necessary to journey north up the Euphrates. From there traders or armies could pass north into Asia Minor or west across northern Syria to Damascus and then on into Canaan where the coastal highway, the Via Maris, provided a pathway to Egypt. An alternate route from Damascus, known as the King's Highway, led south through Transjordan and to the Gulf of Aqaba. This route was more commercial in nature since it gave access to the natural resources of that region and provided a maritime link to the Sinai Peninsula, to the Arabian coast, and to Egypt by means of the Red Sea.

Along the northern coast of Syria lay the powerful seaport city of Ugarit. It dominated the carrying trade in the eastern Mediterranean between 1600 and 1200 BCE, bearing cargoes to and fro from Crete, Cyprus, Greece, the Aegean, and the coast of Asia Minor. Perhaps because of their emphasis on commercial activity, the merchants of Ugarit modified the cumbersome cuneiform script used in Mesopotamia, creating an alphabetic script that increased literacy, contributed to a rich body of literature, and allowed businesses to bypass or weaken the scribal guilds. Such a rich city was a prize and it eventually fell under the hegemony of the Hittite empire during the reign of Suppiluliumas I (1344–1322 BCE) and his successors. The Hittites' efforts to contest with Egypt for control of Syria-Palestine eventually brought Ugarit's navy into the conflict and in the process exhausted the city's resources and contributed to their fall to the Sea Peoples after 1200 BCE.

Naturally, maritime trade did not cease with the demise of Ugarit. Within a few decades, new contenders for this lucrative business appeared at the seaports of Tyre and Sidon, located on the Lebanese coast in an area that will be called Phoenicia. Drawing together the markets already in place in the eastern Levant, Phoenician sailors expanded their reach throughout the Mediterranean Sea and by the end of the ninth century BCE had established trading colonies at Cadiz in southern Spain, on Sardinia, and at Carthage on the North African coast of Tunisia. Never a major military power, Phoenicia created commercial treaties with many other nations, including ancient Israel, that added to their influence (see Solomon's pact with them in 1 Kgs 5).

A number of small Aramaean kingdoms existed in northern Syria. Bordered by mountain ranges to the northwest that separate them from Asia Minor and with a large inland steppe area frequented by pastoral nomadic tribes, Syria extends to the south as far as the northern Galilee region. Ranging from Aleppo in the north to Damascus in the south, the various kingdoms of Syria often operated as commercial and military rivals to the kingdoms of Israel and Judah during the ninth century BCE. Frequently forced into becoming client states by the Assyrian emperors, they and the other small states occasionally were able to form alliances to try and block or slow down Assyrian expansion. One famous Assyrian inscription found on the Kurkh Monolith of Shalmaneser III contains a list of these allied peoples, including King Ahab of Israel, who temporarily stalled the Assyrian army at the Battle of Qarqar in 853 BCE. These alliances, however, quickly evaporated and the small kingdoms fell back into their predatory activities, each trying to obtain territory at the expense of the others (see 1 Kgs 22:1–4; 2 Kgs 6:8–7:20). Among the Aramean rulers most often mentioned in Assyrian texts and in the biblical narrative is Hazael (842–805 BCE), who repeatedly forced the Assyrians to campaign against him in order to suppress his rebellions, and whose military exploits are said to have caused the prophet Elisha to weep in despair (2 Kgs 8:7–15).

Moving into Canaan proper (euphemistically referred to in the biblical text as "from Dan to Beer-sheba"—1 Sam 3:20), the topographic and environmental conditions become extremely varied within the boundaries of a very small region. With north-south dimensions of approximately 150 miles and 60 miles at its widest point (from the Mediterranean coast to the Jordan River), there are several distinct topographical zones. From west to east are four major geographical eco-zones: (1) the Mediterranean coastal plain; (2) a raising plateau region, the Shephelah, traversed east-west by river channels called wadis that are dry much of the year; (3) the spine of the Central Hill Country, running north-south, which consists of Samaria and the Galilee to the north and the Judean Highlands to the south; and (4) the Jordan Rift Valley containing the Jordan River that runs south from the Sea of Galilee into the Dead Sea. To the southeast of the coastal plain and just south of the Judean Highlands, and beside and below the Dead Sea, there is a dry steppe region known as the Negev wilderness that only contains permanent settlements near continuous springs (i.e., Ein-gedi).

Climate is also a major factor affecting the lives of the people throughout this region. Governed by a Mediterranean climatic cycle, with significant rainfall amounts only occurring in the winter months from October to February, the management of water became a critical factor in everyday existence. Harvests were best in the rich valleys between the coastal plain and the Shephelah and in the area south of the Galilee where rainfall amounts were highest. Other portions of the area were not so fortunate. Rainfall levels diminish on the eastern side of the hill country and in the southern steppe areas of the Negev where herding was more prominent. That in turn limited the type of crops that could be grown there and required farmers to become innovative in their adaptation to the environment. For instance, the construction of terraced hillsides were designed to increase arable land and hold moisture in the soil, and the carving out of cisterns allowed them to store water during dry periods of the year.

Given such a variety of inhabited areas and coupled with the difficulties to travel presented by the hill country, it is not surprising that for much of its early history Canaan consisted of small city-states rather than a cohesive nation. Cities like Jericho just north of the Dead Sea took advantage of a continuous water source to promote agriculture and a prime location to control trade routes to and from Transjordan. On the coast, Canaanite cities were established at Gaza, Ashkelon, and Ashdod, but they never became major players in the maritime trade, even after the Philistines invaded the area after

1150 BCE, because they lacked deep-water ports to service large ships close to shore. In the easier climate and topography of the upper highlands, Megiddo and Beth-shean were built to guard and exploit the only major east-west conduit through the hill country, the Jezreel Valley. Of course, Canaanites also had to face the onslaught of armies from Egypt and Mesopotamia that wished to take control of the lucrative business for themselves or wanted free access to the coast to carry out their military campaigns. One inscription by the pharaoh Tuthmosis III (1479–1425 BCE) described the capture of Megiddo as "equal to the capture of a thousand cities."[10] North of the Sea of Galilee, the city of Hazor flourished as a stop on the international caravan route and was mentioned as a major urban site in the eighteenth-century BCE Mari texts.

To the east of the Jordan River is the Transjordanian Plateau. Bisected into separate areas by deep river valleys running east-west, there existed several occupation areas. Running north to south, they are Bashan, Gilead, Ammon, Moab, and Edom. During the Late Bronze period, the region hosted a number of urban centers. However, changes in climate led to a temporary decline and a return to pastoral nomadic life for much of the population until conditions improved and several small kingdoms were established in the thirteenth and twelfth centuries BCE that served as ancient Israel's neighbors and rivals. With relatively large, flat areas available along the plateau, the people herded sheep and goats and were able to maintain a fairly prosperous agricultural existence. They were aided by the trade along the King's Highway, but these small kingdoms never combined politically, and they eventually fell under the hegemony of the Assyrians and the Neo-Babylonians. The biblical account notes the settlement of some of the Israelite tribes in Gilead and Bashan (Num 34:13–15; Joshua 17:1), but it provides mixed reviews about most of the peoples to their immediate east. Some view the Moabites, Ammonites, and

Edomites as friends and allies (2 Sam 17:27–29), but more often they are vilified as enemies (1 Sam 11:1–4) or as allies of their conquerors (Ps 137:7–9).

The Role of Archaeology

Archaeological surveys and excavations in Syria-Palestine over the past century have revealed a great deal of evidence on the settlement of the region, destruction of various sites, and aspects of everyday life during the period from Iron Age I-A to Iron Age III-A (c. 1200–586 BCE). Except in those instances when inscriptional information is available to correlate with the biblical narrative or when datable destruction layers provide a tie to known historical events, much of the data is mute. In many cases, it simply cannot be used to "prove the Bible" or provide a complete reconstruction of activities during a particular time period.[11] Archaeology is also a destructive science, so in those instances when careful records have not been kept by excavators the data are lost forever.

Aside from these obvious limitations, archaeology is useful in determining when particular sites were established, destroyed, and rebuilt. Many villages and towns were continuously occupied for centuries while others had only a short existence before being destroyed or abandoned. These sites, known as "tells" to archaeologists, accumulated occupation layers over time that in some cases resulted in more than twenty separate levels of occupation during the site's history. Interestingly, the areas of occupation on a tell sometimes shifted from one area to another and in some periods only a small portion of a city site was occupied.

It is the task of the archaeological team to review the history of the site by carefully removing these various levels and areas of occupation. Unlike a cake with layers, however, the levels are not perfectly laid on top of another. Instead, there is often disruption of the materials within each level. Sometimes that is a result of erosion or earthquake activity. More often, however, it is caused by the robbing of the building materials from previous levels or the systematic activities of later settlers or their rulers to remove portions of the site to make way for new construction.

With careful attention to what an excavated site can reveal (keeping in mind that much of what may have once existed there is now gone), it is possible to read the levels or time periods of the site. Among the types of evidence that are still available is the location of the site in relation to other settlements, giving archaeologists a sense of settlement patterns, population density, and some of the reasons why the ancient people chose to build in particular places. Nearby agricultural installations such as terraced hillsides, threshing floors, wine and olive oil presses, and cisterns add to the picture of life and the economy in these ancient villages and towns. Also revealed are the styles of architecture associated with typical housing as well as monumental structures such as palaces and temples, and the construction materials that were used.

Within the houses and other structures, a variety of artifactual remains provides additional clues about the people who lived here. Among the most common artifacts are various forms of ceramics that range in size and purpose from large storage jars to handheld oil lamps. Because these objects are subject to breaking or lose their attraction when new types, styles, and shapes are introduced, pottery is produced continuously. By comparing ceramic types and styles of decoration at various sites, it is possible for archaeologists to develop a ceramic chronology for an area or even a time period. The introduction of new forms or foreign styles are indicators of change, commercial activity, and the invasion of an area by new peoples. Spectroscopic examination of the clay from which the objects are made also provides data on their origin (local, regional, or foreign). Also associated with pottery is the use of broken pieces (ostraca) as informal stationary. Many inscriptions have been discovered on these sherds, including letters such as those found at Arad and Lachish dated to the seventh and sixth centuries BCE that describe the activities of the local military garrisons.

Organic remains, including bones, wood, and carbonized grain, also form a portion of the excavators' findings. They can be analyzed using Carbon 14 dating techniques and in some cases they serve as a means of determining the foods in the dead person's diet, dietary preferences, and the degree to which they could store food against famine or siege.[12] In some cases, tombs and even cemeteries have been uncovered and these discoveries have provided information on the types of disease the people suffered, the grave goods that were buried with their dead, their belief in an afterlife, or a veneration of their ancestors.

While time and the elements have destroyed most metal objects, samples of the weapons (swords, spearheads, and arrowheads) they used, as well as cult objects, various types of jewelry, and metal weights indicate their metallurgic skills and the transition from bronze to iron technology. In a similar way, utilitarian stone objects also tell a tale of everyday life. Stone grinders point to the daily custom of crushing grain into flour and loom weights to show how the improvements in technology of the ancient loom made it possible to fabricate clothing. Holding an object like a hand grinder or a sling stone brings to mind a woman's daily hard work to prepare food or a warrior's efforts to defend or attack a city.

As noted, the work of archaeologists throughout the Middle East has contributed a huge mass of data that is now being scientifically and systematically analyzed. From ceramics to the carbonized remains of olive pits found in storage jars and the examination of pollen deposits, the social history of life in ancient Israel is becoming better known. In some cases, archaeologists have discovered inscriptional materials, such as the tenth-century BCE Gezer Almanac, which contains a listing of the agricultural year accompanied by references to the work performed by villagers in Canaan and their celebratory events.

While the discovery of these ancient remains does not answer all of our questions and in particular seldom provides testimony about major events, except in the case of destruction levels when a city is attacked, remains can help to establish a timeframe for settlement, growth, and decline. Combined with the extrabiblical inscriptional materials and the received text of the Bible, we have a starting point for creating probable reconstructions.

With this in mind, the following chapters contain a critical view of the data we currently possess. Sometimes that will mean dismissing something as either irrelevant or even a fraud since there is a huge trade in fake antiquities. It does not mean, however, blinding ourselves to what may prove valuable because it may endanger cherished preconceptions or ideological bias. In other words, it is always the task of historians to follow the data wherever they lead, and to always seek to verify and authenticate findings before making a judgment or a pronouncement.

2

Israel's Earliest Historical Traditions

The Middle and Late Bronze Period

THE ANCESTRAL NARRATIVES FOUND IN Genesis 12–49 and the exodus account (Exod 1–19), including Moses's central role, fall into the category of foundational stories. In fact, the cultural memories of the ancient Israelites do not make up a single story line attributed to authors from some distinct point in antiquity. Instead, they represent a combination of recollections blended together from different periods and by different groups associated with the ethnic group later identified as the Israelites. It is quite likely that these disparate memories have been used or applied in many situations over time. Therefore, it is the task of this chapter to trace the many pathways of memory and the salient features that eventually grew into the completed narratives of the received biblical text.

It does seem a bit ironic that the ancestral narratives describe Mesopotamia as their original home since that area will also become the site of the exile in the sixth century BCE. The lives of Israel's ancestral figures (Gen 11:27–50:26) contain the story of four successive generations. The common narrative thread that binds them together is the establishment of the covenant with God that promises them both land and children. And, as is the case in foundation stories, the ancestral figures must be tested, taught the meaning of their covenant agreement, and tied through ritual and everyday activities to the land of promise. In addition, these stories contain events in both Mesopotamia and Egypt. Since the descendants of the ancestors will eventually settle in Canaan, it is appropriate that they, like the land they will inhabit, are seen as existing physically and culturally between the major powers of antiquity.

The stories about each of these founding fathers and mothers provide a genealogical framework for both the tribes as well as the nation of Israel. In this way all members of the covenantal community are able to trace their lineage back to a common ancestor and can lay claim to the promise of land and children as expressed in the original covenant agreement with Abram/Abraham (Gen 12:1–3; 15:5–21; 17:1–2). Successive narratives describe the activities and struggles of Abraham's heirs and reinforce YHWH's promise. The narratives also contain embedded descriptions of cultural traditions that will serve as precedents for the people's right behavior that distinguishes them from their neighbors and enemies. The stories provide an explanation for the initial migration to Canaan and then to Egypt that will become the basis for the great saving event in Israelite tradition—the exodus event (Exod 1–16) and the giving of the Ten Commandments at Mt. Sinai (Exod 19–20).

The connection between the ancestors and the story of the people's sojourn in Egypt leads up to a further proof of God's covenantal promise. While in Egypt the people grow in numbers and prosperity, are put to "hard labor" by an unnamed pharaoh, and finally are brought "out of Egypt with a mighty hand and an outstretched arm" (Deut 26:5–6). In later tradition, Egypt, the proverbial land of oppression, becomes synonymous with whichever nation is Israel's current national foe (Assyria in Isa 10:24). The metaphorical image of the oppressor Egypt serves quite well, despite the fact that in later, nonepic narratives Egypt played other roles, including erstwhile political ally (2 Kgs 18:21–24; Isa 30:1–2; 31:1), enemy nation (1 Kgs 14:25–26), or economic partner (1 Kgs 10:28; Prov 7:16).

MIDDLE BRONZE AGE CANAAN

Our knowledge of ancient Canaan in the Bronze Age is based on archaeological, environmental, and extrabiblical textual data. Recent advances in the sciences associated with the analysis of pollen samples and other organic remains, including the use of advanced C^{14} techniques, have also contributed to the development of scholarly opinion about the settlement patterns and political character of the Bronze Age. Table 2.1 lists the terms that scholars generally use for the various historical periods in the ancient Near East.

Much of the Early Bronze Age was characterized by a high urban culture. That rich period that saw the construction of pyramids in Egypt and the establishment of vibrant city-states in Mesopotamia eventually collapsed and was

Table 2.1

ARCHAEOLOGICAL PERIODS

Early Bronze, c. 3200–2200
Middle Bronze I or EB/MB, c. 2200–2000
Middle Bronze II-A, c. 2000–1800/1750
Middle Bronze II-B/C, c. 1800–1570
Late Bronze, c. 1570–1200
Iron Age I-A, c. 1200–1140
Iron Age II-A, c. 1140–840
Iron Age II-B, c. 840–701
Iron Age III-A, c. 701–586

Note: Chronology may vary depending on regions. There is no absolute chronology that works perfectly for the entire ancient Near East.

followed by a period of retrenchment throughout the ancient Near East. The demise of this high culture coincides with the First Intermediate Period in Egyptian history and the end of the Sumerian era in Mesopotamia. Among the major factors associated with the end of the Early Bronze period is climate change. Temperature variation and the effect of changes in standard rainfall patterns caused a drop in agricultural production and impacted economic activity, which contributed to the weakening of a culture heavily dependent on large urban centers.[1] Still, archaeological evidence demonstrates that there was some cultural continuity between the Early Bronze and Middle Bronze periods, and not a complete collapse.[2] Major walled urban centers that had existed at Jericho, Ai, and Megiddo during the Early Bronze age show significant decline between 2200 and 1100 BCE, but there is sufficient textual and archaeological evidence to show that, for much of the second millennium BCE, complex village systems did exist in Canaan and there were a number of fairly good-sized towns and cities.

Some of the return to urbanization in the Middle Bronze II period in Canaan followed a pattern marked initially by the establishment or reestablishment of small urban centers along the coast and then over time spread inland by means of the system of wadi channels and natural north-south valleys or passes.[3] In this way, the coastal cities could take advantage of the commerce that followed the Mediterranean coast and also benefit from the natural resources that could be acquired from the inland villages. Still, tracing the settlement patterns during any historical period, as well as the fluctuation of village/city growth and decline, is sometimes a difficult task. It may depend on factors related to "carrying capacity" (the amount of arable land necessary to support a certain population size), to competition with neighboring sites, and to both local and intrusive political factors.[4]

The result of increased trade between Mesopotamia and Egypt during the nineteenth and eighteenth centuries BCE may have also contributed to the revival of large-scale cultivation on the village level that in turn would have helped to supply some of the needs of large cities and could have contributed to population growth. Archaeological evidence shows the introduction of new fortification techniques designed to counteract the introduction of chariot warfare. Finely made bronze weapons and tools also begin to appear.[5] The appearance of administrative centers and palace complexes like that found at Hazor indicates the growth of an elite population in several cities. All this growth suggests the existence of an increasingly vibrant economy. It also helps to explain the prominent mention of Hazor and other Canaanite cities in Egyptian and Mari texts dating to the eighteenth through fifteenth centuries BCE.

During the transition from Middle Bronze IIB to the Late Bronze period, the urban-based culture of Canaan was disrupted by the migration of Hurrians as they streamed south from their destroyed kingdoms in southeastern Asia Minor (modern-day Turkey) and northern Syria (Mitanni). Increased Egyptian interest in the area during the sixteenth century BCE was primarily tied to the coastal towns from Byblos north into Lebanon. To be sure, the campaigns and the diplomatic activities of the pharaohs in that period were aimed in part at efforts to solidify the southern boundaries of Canaan and ensure Egypt's control of the Sinai following the expulsion of the Hyksos invaders about 1550 BCE.[6] But the full conquest of Canaan by Egypt will wait until the fifteenth century BCE and the reign of Tuthmosis III.[7]

The shift to a more concentrated exploitation included the construction of a string of forts by the Egyptians in the northern Sinai and in Canaan proper. Administrative centers and trading compounds were constructed and maintained for nearly three centuries. A well-defined Egyptian presence continued into the Amarna period in the latter half of the fifteenth century BCE. However, letters written by appointed officials in Canaan to the pharaoh Amenophis III and his son Amenophis IV/Akehnaten show an increasing disintegration of effective control over the area and the emergence of local warlords. Stricter control finally was reintroduced during the reign of Ramesses II in the thirteenth century BCE while Canaan served as a buffer zone between Egypt and the Hittite empire in Turkey and northern Syria. That fact and the challenging incursions of the groups collectively referred to as the Sea Peoples (including the Philistines) after 1200 BCE may eventually have contributed to the collapse of Egyptian administrative control over the area by the end of the twelfth century BCE. With the emergence of the Philistine city-states along the coastal plain and in the Shephelah plateau of southwestern Canaan, the region enters a new political and settlement phase that will be discussed in more detail in chapter 3.

Interestingly, the end of the Late Bronze period also seems to have been characterized, at least to an extent, by changes in environmental conditions. Recent examination of pollen data indicates that a dry period occurred in the southern Levant between 1250 and 1100 BCE, the same period when the Near East was disrupted by the incursions of the Sea Peoples. Thus the demise of a number of the Canaanite city-states and the change in settlement patterns in the Central Hill Country may be attributed to both environmental and political upheaval.[8]

ISSUES OF HISTORICITY

Placing the ancestral narratives or the exodus event into a chronological framework is very difficult. Quite frankly, we lack historical or physical landmarks in the stories that would draw them into a specific time period and link them to known historical figures. While it was once traditional for scholars to date the ancestors of ancient Israel to the transition between Early Bronze and Middle Bronze (ca. 2200–1800 BCE) or into the more urbanized Middle Bronze II period of 1800–1500 BCE, that consensus has been set aside because there are no points of linkage other than inference and the biblical account for this position. The writer's ability to invoke cultural realities that might have characterized a particular time period or setting for the ancestral stories does not mean the story is historical.

Making matters even more difficult for historians, there is no mention in these narratives of any known king or major urban site. All of the narratives center on smaller sites or the areas around towns such as Shechem, Bethel, and Hebron. These places have more significance to later Israelite history and they were not considered regional population centers during the Middle Bronze period. Furthermore, there is no suggestion in the stories of an organized Egyptian political or economic presence in Canaan. This omission stands in stark contrast to archaeological and textual evidence, which verifies Egyptian activity in the region during the time in which these stories are placed.[9]

No verifiable historical event is mentioned in the ancestral tales. It is possible that the reference to Hittites (Gen 23:10; 26:34; 27:46) is a confusion with the Hurrians, who are known to have operated within Canaan between 1600 and 1400 BCE, but it may also refer to Hittite migrants following the breakup of the Hittite empire after 1200 BCE. However, this possible identification is only one example of inference. Complicating matters, when direct negotiations do take place with a local ruler, as in the case of Abraham's and Isaac's contacts with Abimelech, the king of Gerar, they are said to occur in the territory of the Philistines (Gen 21:32; 26:8). Yet these references are anachronisms, since the Philistines did not actually settle in Canaan until after 1150 BCE. The list of kings in Gen 14:1–3, the interaction with Melchizedek of Salem (Gen 14:17–20), and the people of Sodom (Gen 14:21–24; 19) do not fit into any known historical period, nor are any of these individuals known outside the biblical text. Efforts to tie one of them (Amraphel of Shinar—Gen 14:9) to the eighteenth-century BCE king of Babylon, Hammurabi, have no substance based on existing information.

Finally, the characters in the ancestral narratives are centered on local household issues and herding practices. The leaders of the urbanized Canaanite city-states and towns would hardly take notice of Abraham and his household except as one more group of seminomadic peoples, who occupy the less settled areas of the region. Only when the stories deal with people at the village level, as in the case of the purchase of the cave of Machpelah near Hebron (Gen 23), is there a sense of cultural understanding between characters engaged in similar economic pursuits.

With regard to the exodus event, again we are faced with a scarcity of data upon which to build or from which to evaluate. Even though we have extensive records from Egypt, none of them offer any evidence of so notable an event as the departure of 600,000 Hebrew slaves and their families. There is no record of these people leaving Egypt in ruins, destroying its army, or their god killing every firstborn child. Scholarly attempts to pare down the story to a scope that might have escaped being noted in Egypt's records are merely speculative. In fact, the only Egyptian record of the existence of a distinct people calling themselves Israel from this general time period is the late thirteenth-century BCE inscription of the pharaoh Merneptah.

Major Themes in the Ancestral Narratives and the Exodus Story

Given that we have no external evidence for the early history of Israel outside of a scriptural account that in many ways contradicts what we do know about Canaan in the Bronze Age, let's examine what evidence these stories contain, so that we can consider when the stories were written and why. While the basic lack of any supportable historical documentation for these characters and events makes it inadvisable to treat the accounts as part of a traditionally reconstructed, historical chronicle that does not mean that the materials are useless or entirely fictitious as some have suggested.[10] They do provide a number of valuable keys to the way in which the earliest periods of Hebrew/Israelite occupation of Canaan were remembered and recounted by later authors. Thus it is possible to take a middle ground between complete acceptance of the biblical materials on faith and complete rejection of them as ahistorical.[11]

Certain concepts are woven throughout the accounts in Genesis and Exodus because they mattered to the writers and audience in the centuries in which the stories were composed. Unpacking these concepts can help us address the question of their value to historians.

1. **Covenant**: It would be impossible to talk about ancient Israel in any time period of its existence without starting with their covenantal relationship with YHWH. Regardless of the historicity of the encounter between Abram and God in Harran and later at various sites in Canaan, the people who eventually refer to themselves as Israel considered that they were a part of a special contract that established them as the "chosen" recipients of a divine promise of land and children. Such a central concept, perhaps the most pervasive in

the biblical text, requires ancestral "roots" and further clarification as the story progresses.

2. **Honor and Shame**: Throughout its existence, ancient Israel was a collective society. As such, each member, from the household level to the clan, to the tribe, and technically to the entire nation were collectively responsible to and for each other's actions. That social attitude manifested as a number of traditions and customs that hinged on the principle of reciprocity and were reflected in a social control mechanism based on seeking honor within the community and avoiding shame or dishonor. It was possible through adherence to the covenant, legal pronouncements, and family customs to accomplish this goal, but the consequences of failure were the weakening and possible annihilation of the household. The way honor and shame are portrayed in these foundational narratives is sometimes quite explicit and sometimes quite apparently implicit, depending on the storyteller's or compiler's emphasis. In fact, since the honor-shame social mechanism is an underlying social feature, it would have been quite jarring to the audience if this social construction was repeatedly violated in a narrative.
3. **Cultural Precedents**: Among the most important purposes of telling and compiling foundational myths is to provide a sense of antiquity to "why we do" or "why we do not do" certain things. Among the items in this category are the prohibition against human sacrifice (Gen 22), the injunction to circumcise all males (Gen 17), adherence to the protocol of hospitality (Gen 18), the call for observance of festivals and other calendared events (Exod 12), and a sense of responsibility for the weakest members of their society (Gen 38). Each of these legal and social precedents attempts

to differentiate the Israelites from neighboring, noncovenantal peoples, and to reinforce honorable or "wise" behavior. In laying this social foundation, the storytellers make it clear that from the beginning of their history their society was attuned to the shaping and promotion of proper behavior.

4. **Significant Cities**: Canaan is a relatively small place. Still, it is marked by a variety of very distinctive environmental and topographic features that influence its climate, settlement patterns, architecture, agricultural endeavors, and economic practices. Within the spatial designation so expansively referred to as "from Dan to Beersheba" (2 Sam 3:10), there are only a few major urban sites with a population over three thousand. The very fact that characters keep coming back to a small number of sites to repeat or commemorate events does suggest a conscious pattern on the part of ancient storytellers and scribes to focus on these places over others. For example, Bethel, a fairly small urban site, appears again and again as a significant location.[12] In the case of the ancestral stories, the authors provide the "first-time" experience of these places that will later function so importantly in the monarchical period. Still, sufficient topographical features are mentioned in the biblical text and some still exist, allowing us to envision the wider ancient geography contained in the narratives.
5. **Relations with Other Nations**: As discussed in chapter 1, Canaan did not exist in a social vacuum. While never developing a major culture of its own that could compete with the super powers of the ancient world, it served an important function as a physical land bridge between Egypt and the cultures of Asia Minor and Mesopotamia. Much of its history can be

characterized based on this important role as a transportation link for economic activity, a buffer zone between empires, and all too often as a battleground. It is not surprising, therefore, to find that the foundational stories about the ancient Hebrews are filled with reference to these other, more powerful nations, and that there are a number of recognizable examples of cultural borrowing. Abram, after all, is initially described as a citizen of Ur of the Chaldees (southern Mesopotamia) and later he moves to Harran (northern Syria) before eventually migrating to Canaan. In order to survive one of the frequent climate-induced famines in Canaan, he and his household travel to Egypt and in a later period it is said that the extended family of Jacob comes to live in Goshen, in the delta region of Egypt. The foundation story of the exodus is dependent on that Egyptian connection, although as we will see below, the story's various components may not be based on the events as described. In short, it would be impossible to write a history of ancient Israel separate from their international contacts, both positive and negative, with the super powers and rival states of the day. While the foreign contacts made in the foundation stories may not be linked to actual historical events, they do express the idea of the mobility of populations, both voluntary and involuntary, that was a fact of life in antiquity.

MEMORY STUDIES AND FOUNDATION STORIES

With this brief introduction to our current understanding of conditions during the Middle Bronze Age, a straightforward caution on the limitations of archaeology, and an outline of major themes in the ancestral narratives, I now wish to address the possible origins of the stories and their usefulness to historians. It is a natural cultural development for a society as it matures or faces national crises to create or revive foundational stories to undergird its sense of self and its cultural uniqueness. These stories are intended to draw on collective memory to provide or reinforce the basic elements of cultural identity and strengthen the bond of solidarity within the community. They usually center on epic events and eponymous or founding heroes, and it may be assumed that they are based at least in part on cultural memories. Of course, for ancient Israel they have been reshaped over time to fit the needs of the people and their leaders during the political changes that occurred between 900 and 600 BCE, and they may only dimly reflect anything approaching historicity. Still, the stories contain information on many aspects of daily life that can assist us to obtain a better understanding of the place that the ancient Israelites occupied, both in ancient Near Eastern history and in the physical space they occupied and claimed as their own.

Memory and acts of remembrance serve as reference points for members of the community. As long as they continue to be remembered, then they remain culturally alive. And they serve as useful data for historians, providing one more source of information on that culture and its development. With that said, there are two facets of memory studies that will serve as guiding principles in this study. First, the role of memory is to remind individuals and the community as a whole that a person or an event is important for us to remember. Second, memory is often an impetus for society to take action to preserve what is considered essential.[13] While those who remember may not have experienced the seminal events associated with their foundation stories, they do remember them as powerful and fascinating aspects of their past. The depth of experience embedded in the story and the vibrant emotions transmitted to them by the storyteller transform each successive generation into recipients of the foundation story. Thus, for instance, by listening and by participating in the ritual of the Passover, the community is allowed to feel the traumatic effects of the forced migration, the devastation of being homeless, and the anxieties of adapting to a new, hostile environment, as well as the emerging hope attached to Moses's leadership and the giving of the law. In this way they are collectively, if only virtually, attached to their ancestors and are able to place themselves into the story.

Collective memories, because they have been vetted and certified as valuable to a community, tend to be more long-lasting and influential. They therefore are considered worth remembering, commemorating, and passing on to future generations as part of the community's process of cultural education and socialization.[14] For a community to effectively retain these collective memories, they must be solidified in the form of cultural artifacts and by means of ritual performances. Among the items that would house these memories for current and future generations would be legal records, textbooks, inscriptions, and sacred scriptures.

A community's memories of its own past therefore function as a means of retelling a set of constitutive events in a convincing fashion and with credible elements. In the process a "master commemorative narrative" is generated and promoted.[15] Such a narrative, however, remains subject to change, modification, or reshaping as the need for that narrative shifts in much the same way that market branding is refreshed periodically to maintain product consciousness. Thus certain events or characters may obtain greater or lesser emphasis in the story, depending on the need for reciting or referencing a particular portion of the overall narrative.

For our purposes in the discussion of the premonarchic period, there are some memories that are so well known or so important to the people's ethos that memorialization clearly had become institutionalized and therefore was less subject to transformation or manufacture. In these cases, a much greater effort would have to be made to convince the people to give up or radically change something that they considered to be a basic facet of their identity. An argument could be made that the story of the exodus was such a solidified foundation story. It seems almost inconceivable that a people would choose to create and perpetuate a foundation myth in which they lived for centuries as slaves in a foreign land. Setting that in juxtaposition with the saving acts of a deity, who has chosen to "bring them out of Egypt" (Exod 20:2), transforms a shameful beginning into an empowered future that allows for a multitude of adaptations designed to fit Israel's changing political situation in later time periods. It also establishes a case for a deity, who is both interactive and distinct among all the gods of the Near East. Such a conclusion better fits the postexilic period's efforts to define YHWH, but it may also have strong roots in a tradition of the saving acts of a divine warrior and creation god. Either way, the exodus story is a strong cultural component, too well known, too often retold to be an entirely late literary creation.

Despite the importance attached above to the retention of memories as a source of information about the past, it must be admitted that some memories are intentionally manufactured. These artificial memories spring into being at the moment when they are created and then publicly voiced in order to serve the purposes of the author or those he or she serves. They quite likely draw on fragments of reality or earlier more credible memories that then blossom into a full-blown set of images and stories as their credibility grows.

For example, the story of the archetypal hero, whether he be Gilgamesh or Moses, draws on a set of type-scenes like a miraculous birth narrative, the miraculous passage through a sea of death, or saving the people from oppression or defeat through divine intervention. Ultimately, the reality of what a hero may have actually accomplished and his human failings become clouded or submerged into the overriding narrative that creates his bigger-than-life persona. His value to the community is as an eponymous hero, and if any flaws are retained in his story, then they also must serve some purpose in relating the values of the creative community or at least as a form of entertainment. By using familiar personages or events, the creators of manufactured memory can piece together or modify the collective memory to serve their purposes. It must at first require the imposition of authority or the collaboration of authority figures to override any counter voices, who "remember" another version, but that can be done with enough time and effort. Then, once the new portion of the foundation myth becomes normative, it is merged with and indistinguishable from the meta-narrative from which it drew a portion of its substance.

Memory studies acknowledge that what we too often refer to as history is a memory of a memory, reshaped and manufactured to satisfy current (i.e., the time of the compiler) cultural requirements.[16] No story remains the same for long. As long as there is a new generation of storytellers and a new set of interpreters to analyze or reframe the story, it will continue to change or take on new meaning. Thus we have in the received biblical text a version, at least, of how effective the melding of traditions and memories has been over time. It is therefore the reconstruction process that will interest us here. Not that every revision can be traced to its origins, but at least it may be possible to investigate the social forces that influenced the shaping and reshaping of the story.

ANCESTRAL NARRATIVES AND ANCIENT ISRAEL'S HISTORICAL TRADITIONS

Geographical Associations

Given the effort made by the ancient compilers of the stories over a number of generations to present them in a fairly logical and chronological order, perhaps the place to start then is with the references to Mesopotamia. Abram and Sarai are first mentioned as residents of Ur of the Chaldees (Gen 11:31a). Immediately, we are faced with a significant anachronism since the Chaldees are a Babylonian ethnic group that does not appear in Assyrian records in that region until the ninth century BCE and is associated with King Nebuchadnezzar II, who destroyed Jerusalem in 586 BCE and took a large portion of the population of Judah into exile. That indicates that the traditions of Mesopotamian origin for the founding couple of Israel are associated with the exilic period and the desire on the part of the exiles to return home.

However, the association of Abram and his household with the northern Syrian town of Harran (Gen 11:31b) suggests that some memories of Mesopotamia may not go back much farther than the exile. The region of Harran, well documented in the eighteenth-century BCE Mari administrative letters, is known for its pastoral nomadic tribes and fluid population. Better than a southern urban center, Harran serves the purposes of the biblical narrative as a good staging area and transit point from which to undertake a journey to Canaan. Unfortunately, the narrative contains a gap and fails to provide any information on the route taken by Abram's migrating household other than the point of departure and the point of arrival at Shechem (Gen 12:4–6). For the historian, narrative gaps are a frustration. In this case, it works to the advantage of the storyteller to demonstrate the unwavering faithfulness of the hero to the original audience. In this way Abram is portrayed as willingly accepting the challenges of leaving familiar territory and setting out into the unknown with his family.

Why then is the city of Shechem the first place in Canaan mentioned? If Abram followed the traditional caravan route, he would have seen and perhaps visited many towns and cities, including Damascus, Hazor, Megiddo, and others. Even as a household traveling with flocks of sheep and goats, they would have had to stop to graze their animals, seek permission for the use of pasturage or plowed fields, and they would have encountered other peoples along their route of travel. But it is significant that Shechem (Tell Balatah) appears first. Shechem (about forty miles north of Jerusalem) has a long history of settled existence, including as a major urban site during the Middle Bronze III period (ca. 1650–1500 BCE), and as an Egyptian administrative center during the Amarna period (ca. 1400–1300 BCE). Its primary importance for Israelite history comes during the monarchy period (1 Kgs 12:1, 25) when it serves as an administrative and cultic center for the northern kingdom of Israel until the Assyrian conquest in 721 BCE. In later periods, Shechem is associated with the Samaritans, and nearby Mt. Ephraim served as a major cultic site (John 4:20).

It is therefore possible that the answer to the question may be based on the political agenda of a northern kingdom storyteller's attempt to add authority to Shechem at the expense of Jerusalem during the time of the divided monarchy. Equally possible, however, is that this story is being told in the seventh century BCE after the destruction of the northern kingdom by people interested in uniting the land under either King Hezekiah or Josiah.

Still, there are other stopping points for Abram and his household and some of them are intimately tied to both Judah and the northern kingdom of Israel. To a certain extent that mitigates complete control of the narrative by a single political or theological influence, but it does provide insight into how the stories were shaped to serve the purposes of authorities in later time periods. Among the sites that Abram visited are Bethel (Gen 12:8; 13:3), Hebron (Gen 13:18), and Beer-sheba (Gen 21:31–32). It should be noted that at each of these places Abram/Abraham makes camp, builds an altar or plants a tree, and calls on the name of YHWH. In this way, the storyteller creates specific geographical boundaries for the land given to Abram in the covenant, and introduces the worship of YHWH for the first time in that region.

Possibly as important as the cultic pathway created by Abram and later reinforced by his ancestral successors (Isaac at Beer-sheba—Gen 26:23–25; Jacob at Shechem—Gen 33:18–20) is the generational association of the ancestors with Hebron. Hebron also is closely tied in the biblical narrative to the House of David. It is here that David first ruled the tribe of Judah as their chief (2 Sam 2:1–4) and it is to Hebron that the tribal elders come to proclaim David king of the fledgling coalition of tribes calling themselves Israel (2 Sam 5:1–3). Hebron, while a centralized community within the tribal territory of Judah, serves as an appropriate spot for David's administrative center. However, the site's previous ties to the ancestors added greater authority, both in terms of managing an extended "household" of affiliated clans and in terms of its covenantal links to the land.

Sometimes Hebron's location is also keyed to the vicinity of the "oaks of Mamre" (Gen 13:18; 14:13; 18:1), but central to the importance of this site is the purchase of the cave of Machpelah as a communal tomb (Gen 23). The extended transactional dialogue between Abraham and Ephron the Hittite provides a remarkable example of bargaining, but even more remarkable is the sale of land to an outsider. To be sure, the bargaining is one-sided since the seller understands Abraham's immediate need to bury his dead, but the presence of the town elders may have kept it a civil exchange and the price, while exorbitant, once paid ensured that the landless household of Abraham at last had a legal claim to the land promised in the covenant. There may not be any more important precedent than this one since it legitimizes ownership and presents a creditable justification for returning to that land even after long absences (see Jacob's request to be buried there [Gen 49:29–33] and Joseph's request to be buried in the land sworn to the ancestors [Gen 50:24–25; Exod 13:19]). The precedent of allegiance to the land is then echoed in the prophet Jeremiah's purchase/redemption of land from his relative in Jer 32:1–15.

As will be discussed in more detail below, Egypt is also featured in the ancestral narratives, as a place both of danger and of sanctuary. Abram's journey to Egypt is in line with the movement of "Asiatics" as they are labeled in Egyptian texts into the delta region to purchase food in times of famine (Gen 12:10). While a case could be made that the Egyptians generally abhorred contact with the "miserable" Asiatics (Merikare, COS 1.35:64), there is sufficient evidence to show that in several periods foreign workers, mercenaries, and slaves (prisoners of war) were absorbed into the Egyptian culture.[17] The precedent provided by Abram's trickery, fooling the divine ruler of Egypt into thinking Sarai is his sister (12:11–20), serves two purposes. It reinforces the underdog motif, allowing the weaker party to scheme and lie in order to gain an advantage. And, on a larger scale, it displays the power of Abram's god even in a physical context in which Egypt should have the upper hand. The later precedent foreshadows the context between Moses/YHWH and pharaoh in the exodus account.

The migration of Jacob's extended family to Goshen provides another link to a practice that may have been associated with the Hyksos conquest and occupation of Lower Egypt in the seventeenth century BCE. While there are no historical references in Egyptian texts to a specific group identified as Israel or with any of the ancestral households settling in the Nile delta region, the storyteller may well have been aware of such practices by Asiatics. It would have been easy enough to create a well-crafted narrative such as the Joseph story that would place the Hebrew tribes in Egypt and therefore provide the foundation for the subsequent exodus story. Is that a manufactured memory or a shaping of disparate traditions? We have no way of knowing for sure, but since the exodus is such a central event in Israelite tradition, it makes sense that the compilers of the narratives would wish to add an ancestral precedent for settlement and subsequent liberation from Egypt.

These stories associated with specific geographical locations are important cultural precedents and will serve as the foundation for many later events set at these places of residence by the ancestors and their descendants. The appearance of these sites in stories associated with antiquity also will become the basis for the scribal practice of geographic reiteration in later periods. While the stories of the ancestors do not portray them as building cities, it is understood by the ancient audience that the regular presence near urban sites by pastoral groups serves as a tribal legacy for the future use of the land and its resources in order to sustain their households and flocks. Then, in later periods the covenantal claim is paired with the long-standing and regular association with the land as the basis for the conquest and construction of cities by the Israelites.

Foundational Social Traditions

In relating the stories about the ancestors, an important function of the narratives is to provide a foundation for social customs and traditions. Tying them to the ancestors gives them greater authority and adds to the socialization process that is a part of every culture's basic introduction to proper behavior. When such customs are also sanctioned by a deity, they take on even greater authority and become the basis for enforcing the honor-shame paradigm. While it is not possible to tie the events in which these social requirements are introduced to specific time periods or historical events, their appearance in the ancestral narratives at least suggests their importance to the culture and its identity.

How then do we differentiate between social customs that are basically universal in the ancient Near East and those specific social customs that are introduced in the ancestral narratives that set them apart from other peoples and therefore serve as precedents for Israel in the future? To begin with, it must be established that the sanctioned actions, activities, celebrations, and social mandates are in fact unique or are intimately tied to membership in the community. For example, every ancient culture in the Near East outlawed wanton murder, theft, false witness, and adultery. However, there are instances in the ancestral narratives in which the normal injunction against lying (bearing false witness) is violated and even celebrated as a contest between gods (Gen 12:11–20; 20:2–7). That suggests that a measure of proper behavior for the storyteller is not only situational, but also a reflection of power relationships and a pervasive theme in the narratives in which the "underdog" is given greater license in order to survive threats.

Turning to less anomalous examples of social behavior, the practice of circumcising males, while not entirely unique to the Israelites since it is also practiced by the Egyptians, serves as a prime example of ritualized behavior associated with communal membership. This divinely mandated operation (Gen 17:10–14) involves a relatively minor surgical procedure, which is required of all males at least eight days old, functions as a form of sacrificial offering, an easily identifiable example of ritual scarring, and is a means of labeling nonmembers.

Repeatedly the pejorative term "uncircumcised" is applied to males considered unacceptable for marriage (Gen 34:14), a ritually unclean person (Exod 12:48), and for the Philistines in general (Judg 14:3; 1 Sam 17:26). References to circumcision continue to appear in the literature of the settlement and early monarchy period (Judg 15:18; 1 Sam 31:4; 2 Sam 1:20). In the prophetic literature the term is used to describe all foreign nations (Jer 9:26; Ezek 32:19; Isa 52:1). What that suggests is a formal acceptance of circumcision as a required practice by the Israelites, reinforced by its institution in the ancestral account. The evolution of its metaphorical usage takes place as Israel ceased to struggle militarily with its neighbors and instead set itself aside from all other nations because of their claim to a unique covenantal pact with YHWH as the basis of their identity.

There is some evidence that human sacrifice, especially that of children, was a feature of Canaanite worship and serves as the focus of the story of the sacrifice of Isaac in Gen 22:1–19. While playing on the same "faithful servant" theme that began the ancestral wanderings, it also presents a case for divinely mandated substitutionary sacrifice of animals rather than humans.[18] There may also be a case being made here, at least based on tradition if not fact, associating Abraham and this crisis event with Jerusalem/Moriah (see 2 Chron 3:1). That identification cannot, however, be established with any certitude.

More important to the ancestral narratives and to their influence on later Israelite cultural practices is the tension built up in the story, leaving the audience to imagine the turmoil in the minds of both father and son and perhaps gasping as the knife is raised over the bound child. For later audiences, the demand for a human sacrificial victim and the apparently callous response on Abraham's part to give up the long-awaited son and heir could have been deemed outrageous. But then of course they knew the ending. There is a pun embedded in the Hebrew text that plays on the provision of a sacrifice and the word for ram that adds a measure of entertainment and suggests a careful retooling of the story to create this effect. Ultimately, it provides the cultural and legal precedent for prohibiting human sacrifice by the Israelites (compare the demand for the first-born in Exod 13:2; 22:29), differentiating them from their Canaanite neighbors (see Micah 6:6–8). It also provides the basis for instances of shock literature in which human sacrifice by Israelites and by their enemy neighbors (Mesha of Moab—2 Kgs 3:5b–25) does take place in later periods (Jephthah's daughter—Judg 11:29–40; Ahaz's son—2 Kgs 16:3).

While better articulated in legal statements (Exod 22:21–27; Deut 24:12–15, 17) and in wisdom literature (Prov 14:31; 19:17), concern for the powerless and the poor in society has its precedents in the ancestral narratives as well. Abram's rescue of Lot after the city of Sodom is attacked and its people taken as slaves (Gen 14) demonstrates the strength of responsibility to kin. The recognition by Judah that he had wronged his widowed daughter-in-law Tamar (Gen 38:1–26) sends a signal that the powerful should not ignore the legal rights of the weakest members of the community. At the heart of this social imperative, however, is the insistence that God also is expected to act in a just manner toward all people, even those not within the covenantal community.

THE EXODUS EVENT

History or Collective Memory?

The question remains whether the exodus, either as described in the biblical text or through an evaluation of extrabiblical and archaeological data, can be verified as a facet of ancient Israel's history. This question has sparked enormous debate among scholars, who are willing to entertain the idea that there is some measure of historical character to the story. They attempt to gather data and circumstantial evidence to posit possible dates that range from the mid-fifteenth century BCE to the period after the invasion of the Sea Peoples in the twelfth century BCE.[19] Other scholars have branded the exodus story a myth, but one that may have some historical roots.[20] Certainly, there are quite a number of literary parallels, including the Nile changing to blood and the drowning of a pharaoh's army.[21] However, in what would be considered historical documents, we do not have any direct references to the exodus of the Hebrews from the perspective of the Egyptians. Only the Merneptah Stele (1208 BCE), which includes a reference to the "people" of Israel living in Canaan at the end of the thirteenth century, suggests a direct connection with the biblical narrative.

Beyond that, it is only possible to point to a few Egyptian texts that verify the existence of "Asiatics" in Egypt during the second millennium BCE. For example, Papyrus Anastasi VI (4.11–6.5; dating to c. 1209 BCE) mentions Shosu bedouins being granted entrance into the area of the Wadi Tumilat (the eastern end of the delta) and specifically to the "Lakes of Pithom" to pasture their flocks.[22] But there are no ledgers detailing the names of Israelites in this text, nor are the members of this Semitic group referred to as slaves or engaged in construction activities. All this and a few pieces of archaeological data (a "Proto-Israelite" four-room house near Thebes dating to the mid-twelfth or early eleventh century BCE) demonstrate is the presence of Semitic groups associated with Transjordan and Canaan who are said to be living and working in Egypt during the Middle Bronze period.

From the perspective of the biblical text, references to Pi-Rameses and Pithom (see Exod 1:11) do suggest that the compilers of the biblical tradition were familiar with some late

Ramesside (20th Dynasty) Egyptian topographic names (Pi-Ramesse, Pi-Atum, Tjeku, and Pa-Tjuf). That knowledge could be the basis for the construction of their itinerary of events. It could strengthen the argument that the exodus trek begins from the Egyptian site of Pi-Ramesse (Qantir; near Avaris, Tell el-Dabʿa), crosses the Ballah Lakes system (a possible location for the Reed Sea/Yam Suph crossing), and thus avoids the string of Egyptian fortifications along the coastal highway known as the Way of Horus.[23]

The biblical reference to this international highway as the "Way of the Philistines" (Exod 13:17) has sometimes been judged to be an anachronism since the Philistines did not occupy the area until after 1150 BCE. However, if these geographic references in the biblical account come from the late Ramesside period, then that would be in keeping with the other early eleventh-century BCE data and Philistine settlement.[24] In sum, current information suggests that the scribal compilers of the exodus narrative were somewhat familiar with Egyptian topography or at least with Egyptian texts dating to the twelfth and eleventh centuries BCE that contain these place-names, and may have used them to create a story plausible to their original audience. That also serves as a plausible argument to tie the origins of the biblical tradition to the monarchy period rather than to the Persian or Hellenistic era.

However, it also should be noted that the identification of ancient sites does have its difficulties. The use of a particular place-name can shift from one site to another in later periods. Stones taken from these older cities that contain the inscriptions and names of earlier rulers can cause a new city to be mistaken for the older one. Thus, unless there is enough verifiable evidence provided by excavation and lexical data, one needs to be careful in drawing conclusions.

Given these various pieces of data on which to build a hypothesis, what remains is a debate between scholars over the possible historicity of the exodus event. Some scholars raise the possibility that the exodus story does contain some memories from a time when the Hebrews or Proto-Israelites once lived in Egypt and may have either escaped an oppressive situation or were expelled along with other Semitic peoples.[25] Such a well-crafted story with a powerful ending that favors YHWH and the Israelites explains the retelling of the story. Since it also contains details that match known geographic features in Egypt, as noted above, and references to familiar elements of Egyptian religion and culture added appeal for the ancient Israelite audience. But telling a story is not enough.

For it to truly capture the imagination and become solidified in the collective memory of a people, it must be commemorated regularly in ritual. The inclusion of the Passover festival in legal statutes and associated with major events in Israelite history reinforces its importance and solidifies its details to the point where it becomes increasingly difficult to change them (Lev 23:5; Num 9:2–14; Deut 16:1–6; Josh 5:10; 2 Kgs 23:21–23). Then it becomes the charter for adherence to the covenant that finds its way into the injunctions of prophets (Ezek 45:21) and into the speeches of characters in the New Testament period like Stephen (Acts 7:20–43).

Tracing the story along the pathway of tradition, however, is not an entirely satisfying solution to the question of historicity. If an exodus-like event did occur, can it be posited within a set of circumstances that does not require a period of enslavement and a physical escape from Egyptian soil? One suggestion that has been made is that Proto-Israelites experienced a different type of oppression, but in Canaan, not Egypt. We have archaeological data, administrative and inscriptional documentation that attests that during the period from ca. 1500 to 1200 BCE Egypt maintained a strong presence in Canaan. During that time, they exploited its resources and peoples, including deporting some of them back to Egypt to serve as a labor force. When Egypt eventually lost effective control of the region, the subject peoples of Canaan were released from Egyptian oppression.

In this scenario, the withdrawal of Egyptian administrative control over Canaan toward the end of the beleaguered 20th Dynasty (ca. 1100 BCE) becomes the impetus for the exodus story. As Egypt withdraws within its borders under the continuing threat of the Sea Peoples, the peoples of Canaan, including the newly arrived Philistines, were given the opportunity to establish their own distinctive cultures, build new settlements, and not have to answer to the centuries-long, arbitrary demands of the Egyptians for resources and men. Plus they would not have to face the possibility of forced deportation to serve as laborers in Egypt. Although not coming in a heroic mass migration, liberation was achieved and could easily be ascribed by the Israelites to divine intervention. It could also serve as further proof of the covenantal agreement between the people of Israel and their god.[26] In other words, it is not necessary to set the exodus in Egypt at all. The story therefore hinges on an end to a long period of oppression and a separation from those oppressors, allowing the people to at last take root in the Promised Land.

What then is the solution to the question of the historicity of the exodus account? At this point, quite simply, there is no definitive solution or consensus. We only can speculate on the likelihood of various scenarios and dates, and we must keep an open mind to the possibility that new data will shed light on whether any portion of the biblical narrative is tied to actual events. And it is worthwhile to examine how this well-constructed narrative has helped to shape Israelite identity and served as a reassurance of divine intervention when the political pendulum once again places Israel in a position of oppression or potential extinction as a people.

The Origin of the Exodus Story

Then how much truth does a foundation story need to contain to be recognized as of value to its audience? A story that ignores the basic social values of the audience is simply too fantastic for them to believe. If it is too cavalier in changing the details of well-known historical events, it is less likely to be accepted or be retained in their collective memory except as an entertaining fiction. Therefore, what is it about the exodus story that allows it to not only abide in the collective consciousness, but be intentionally memorialized in public and private rituals and cited in popular psalms (see Ps 78:12, 43, 51; 80:8; 81:10; 114:1; 135:8–9)? It is, of course, possible that the exodus story initially was only associated with the traditions of a single small group that subsequently merged with other peoples. The melting pot of the new settlements in the highlands of Canaan during the Late Bronze Age must have brought together many stories and blended them into new epic form. Furthermore, the emergence of Israel as a nation could have contributed to the adoption of the exodus story as a national foundation story.[27] That broadening of purpose and appeal, however, could have required major revision and an imposition of centralized authority in order to make it relevant and acceptable to all of the tribes and clans that eventually coalesced into the national fabric, the so-called mixed crowd (Exod 12:38).

But the question remains: when and why did the ancient Israelites create this particular foundation story? If its origins are not tied to some point in the twelfth century or earlier, then is the tenth century during the early monarchic period a likely point for its creation? Or is it a reflection of the northern kingdom's attempt to separate ideologically from Jerusalem and the House of David?[28] Or is it part of the eighth-century prophets' triads against the division of the kingdom by Jeroboam and his successors in Israel? Does it tie into their message that Israel's decline is based on the installation of golden calves at Dan and Bethel (1 Kgs 12:26–30) and the people's failure to adhere to their obligations under the covenant (Hos 8:11–14; Amos 3:1–11)?

For instance, Hosea identifies "Egypt" as the place of Israel's exile after their immanent destruction by the Assyrians (Hos 8:13). In this way Egypt takes on the metaphorical identity as the seat of oppression. By making this equation, however, the prophet may also be offering hope for another example of divine intervention (i.e., the exodus from Egypt). For his metaphorical reference to work, however, there would have had to be an awareness of the exodus tradition in Israel prior to Hosea so that his audience could both grasp his warning and appreciate the symbolism.

Even if the kingdom of Israel knew and commemorated the exodus story that does not mean that the kingdom of Judah did as well. There is almost a complete absence of any mention of the exodus account in the annals of the kings of Judah prior to the eighth century. The only direct reference to Moses (other than in the context of law) and the exodus experience is found in Solomon's dedication of the Jerusalem temple (1 Kgs 8:16, 21, 51–53, 56). When it does begin to appear, the northern kingdom has been destroyed by the Assyrians in 721 BCE and Judah has experienced at least two Assyrian invasions in 711 BCE and 701 BCE. It also is likely that refugees from Israel had found their way to Judah and may have brought the exodus story with them. It may well have resonated with the people of Judah, who had seen God's punishment firsthand and could understand how this disaster could be ascribed to their failure to keep their covenant obligations (see 2 Kgs 17:7–18). These experiences could then explain the appearance of references in the annals of Judah's kings justifying YHWH's anger against their nation (2 Kgs 21:13–15). It could also provide the traditional foundation needed for Micah's (6:4; 7:15), Jeremiah's

(2:6; 7:25), and Ezekiel's (20:5–11) use of the exodus tradition to frame Judah's increasingly desperate situation?

The question then arises whether the revived exodus story became a theological vehicle used by the retrospective historian, the Deuteronomist. That could help to explain Samuel's argument against the people's demand for the monarchy, construing it as a rejection of the collective memory of the divine warrior's saving acts in bringing them out of Egypt (1 Sam 8:8; 10:18; 12:6–8). The Deuteronomist's editing of events associated with Solomon's dedication of the new temple (1 Kgs 8:21, 53) and YHWH's fidelity to the House of David (1 Kgs 8:16) could then explain why the exodus appears in only these seminal episodes.

Solomon's dedicatory speech, using language that evokes the memory of YHWH's rescue of the people from Egypt, "from the midst of the iron-smelter" (1 Kgs 8:51) that is then repeated in Jeremiah's sixth-century BCE message (Jer 11:4) also points to Deuteronomistic editing of the details of this event. Plus, it is quite possible that the Deuteronomist intentionally compares the theodicy of failure associated with the fall of Samaria and the positively described reform efforts of Hezekiah (2 Kgs 17:21–23; 18:3–8) and Josiah (2 Kgs 23:21–23). It is not surprising to find that Josiah not only ordered the cleansing of the Jerusalem temple, but also reinstituted the celebration of the Passover, a clear tie back to the exodus event and its theme of new beginnings.

The other alternative is that the exodus story is a convenient narrative vehicle either created or recycled during the exilic period. If that is the case, then Second Isaiah's (52:3–6) pairing of the story of the Hebrews in Egypt alongside the more recent Assyrian oppression functions very well as a reassurance of the eventual end to Babylonian captivity. Based on this possible origin of the exodus story, it could have been created to revitalize the hopes of the exiles, telling them that they will indeed be freed to return to Jerusalem and once again be able to claim the Promised Land (Isa 11:16; Zech 10:10). Or, if it is a fifth-century BCE, postexilic creation, it may have been intended as a means of encouraging a reluctant ex-patriot community to leave their comfortable homes in Mesopotamia or Persia and return to Judah to rebuild the nation and the Jerusalem temple (Hag 2:5). The story could even have been designed to provide encouragement to the communities in the Egyptian diaspora (Isa 19:16–17).[29]

Finally, if the exodus account is not a late creation, is there any possibility that an account of centuries-long Egyptian oppression and the exodus are actual events that have survived throughout Israelite tradition by means of memorial commemoration? The answer to that question will have to be left to archaeologists, historians, and philologists. In their future examination of the text and physical data, they may someday be able to determine the reality of the exodus account and the role of Moses in the history of ancient Israel. At this point, using current data, it seems unlikely that the exodus occurred in precisely the way that the story has been crafted in the received text.

Exodus as a Foundation Story

At what point does the memory of events begin to function as a national epic or a foundation story? The exodus story is retained in collective memory through commemoration in an annual festival (Deut 16:1–12), is taught to children (Exod 13:14; Deut 6:20–21; 32:7), and is referenced as a reliable theodicy to authenticate legal injunctions (Deut 24:17–18) or to provide a context when similar dangers to the nation present themselves (Hos 11:1–5; Jer 32:20–23).

The attributes of this story that give it the ability to remain a part of the collective memory from one generation to the next allow it to resonate within the community and add to their collective sense of identity. It is entertaining and it provides a fairly simple message that can continue to relate to the basic value system of the community down through the centuries. Although the exodus story begins with the willful enslavement and oppression of the Hebrews, its resolution becomes the cardinal example of God's response to free a captive people and restore their fortunes as the covenantal community. This remarkable saving event is so powerful it has been codified and recited in later periods as an assurance that the nation is never without hope of once again experiencing divine intervention.

To explore this aspect of the exodus story, let us set aside the issue of its possible historicity and examine the possible purposes for the compilation of the exodus narrative and its role as a foundation story. At the heart of this endeavor is the marked emphasis within the story of God's numerous saving acts that lead to the Hebrews' liberation from Egypt. That narrative is then coupled with a series of episodes in the book of Exodus in which the escapees are given provisions, protection by the divine warrior, and continual reminders of God's presence on their way to the Promised Land (Exod 16; 17:8–16; 33:7–11).

Interestingly, the joy and sense of relief associated with the exodus soon evaporates and therefore the remainder of the narrative, principally found in the books of Numbers and Deuteronomy, contains a "complaint motif" that signals the lack of faith on the part of the people (Exod 15:24; 17:3; Num 14:2), and it becomes the basis for their relegation to the wilderness for the next two generations (Num 14:26–35; forty years) and a culling of the rebellious in a series of harsh divine manifestations of power (Num 16; 21:1–9). Only Moses's intervention on the people's behalf prevents a mass extermination of these ungrateful escapees.

Throughout this secondary narrative, Moses is repeatedly forced to address a wrathful YHWH, make excuses, and ask for mercy for the people despite their failings. These postexodus events, including the Golden Calf episode (Exod 32), take the luster off of what YHWH has accomplished in bringing them out of Egypt. But they also showcase the fact that remembrance has a reverse side—forgetting. A story in which the Hebrews who had experienced the exodus never complained about the conditions in the wilderness and never doubted YHWH's intention to bring them to a better land might well be considered too fanciful. However, a story that provided a foundational pathway to a different sort of redemption predicated on repentance for sin and a return to fidelity to the covenant could function very well in an imperfect world.

This secondary story line set in the wilderness therefore becomes particularly important in later periods of Israelite history. When the nation and its leaders began to dabble in international politics (see Isa 36:4–7; 2 Kgs 23:28–30) and to blend the worship of YHWH with Canaanite and Assyrian deities (Jer 2:26–28; Ezek 8) the prophets use these practices to explain the destruction of cities and eventually the overthrow of both Israel and Judah by foreign powers (Jer 25:1–14). Thus the theodicy for the fall of Israel to Assyria (Hos 11:1–5) and Judah to the Babylonians is tied to the failure of the people to obey the covenant even though YHWH "showed signs and wonders in the land of Egypt" and "brought your people Israel out of the land of Egypt with signs and wonders" (Jer 32:20–23).

Even with the troubles associated with the wilderness wanderings, the original meaning of the exodus event remains intact. For it is clear that to say "remember the exodus" also means remember the covenant.[30] As a result, in Israelite tradition a theologically based, scribal catch-phrase is used to refer to YHWH's saving act of "bringing the people out of Egypt" (Num 22:5; 23:22; Deut 4:34; Lev 19:36; 1 Kgs 8:9, 16; Ps 81:10; Jer 7:22; Amos 9:7). Furthermore, obedience to the law and the perpetuation of ritual worship are justified by reference to the period of slavery in Egypt. Examples of this practice include the reasoning for the festival of unleavened bread (Exod 13:3); prohibition against enslavement of fellow Israelites (Lev 25:39–42); observance of the Sabbath (Deut 5:12–15); and the mandate to ensure that the weak in society (resident aliens, widows, and orphans) are granted justice under the law (Deut 24:17–18).

The storytellers and compilers of the exodus narrative also perpetuate the memories of divine intervention by placing them in the mouths of non-Israelites. In this way it is demonstrated that these sacred memories are not held by the Israelites alone, but are shared and repeated by neighboring peoples. For example, when Rahab speaks to Joshua's spies after they enter Jericho, she tells them that "we have heard how the Lord dried up the water of the Red Sea before you when you came out of Egypt, and what you did to the two kings of the Amorites that were beyond the Jordan, to Sihon and Og, whom you utterly destroyed" (Josh 2:10). Her speech serves as further recognition of the power of YHWH by non-Israelites. By extension, it also gives authority to Israelite claims to distinctiveness as the chosen people, who have been directed by God to begin their conquest of the Promised Land. However, the Israelites are also starkly reminded that they have agreed to serve a god who others recognize as "God in heaven above and earth below" (Josh 2:11; see Exod 19:3–8).

Moses: Hero and Lawgiver

To complete our assessment of the exodus story, it is essential that we also examine the role of Moses. Legendary heroes, like ancestral figures, may have little to do with actual historical events. To date, no extrabiblical record of Moses has been found. None of the events that he initiated, such as the contest with the unnamed pharaoh and the sequence of ten plagues (Exod 7:14–12:32), have been authenticated through textual or archaeological discoveries. Even the exact location of Mt. Sinai cannot be verified. Certainly, it is possible to say that the wastes of the Sinai wilderness could swallow up any physical evidence of the passage of the Hebrews, even if they languished there for forty years. But the absence of data is not an acceptable way to trace the history of a people.

Heroes such as Moses are often featured in stories set in transitionary or unstable periods. During an era of political uncertainty, destruction of established urban centers, and the emergence of new ethnic groups, it becomes necessary for champions to appear, who will restore a sense of stability and provide a pathway to the creation of an ordered society. The Israelite epic would, of course, have to feature a hero chosen by divine intervention and would in many respects be a bigger-than-life character, who champions the covenantal agreement and becomes a precedent-setter for later Israelite rulers. Moses fills this role as a remarkable, multifaceted hero, who is able to transcend the model of the self-aggrandizing and self-indulgent, semi-divine figure celebrated in the Gilgamesh epic. Interestingly, Moses is also portrayed as very human with simple failings and anxieties. For instance, he has to be reminded by his father-in-law Jethro that he cannot spend all of his time judging the disputes of his people. That experience leads him to establish a precedent of delegating authority to tribal elders (Exod 18:13–26). Similarly, when an overwhelmed Moses calls on God for respite from the complaints of the people, YHWH commands him to share his responsibilities with the Seventy Elders (Num 11:10–30).

Some of the precedents and elements of the exodus narrative have their roots in ancient Near Eastern epic literature. Foundation stories and heroic epics often borrow or include well-known themes and heroic deeds. For example, Moses's very distinctive birth narrative (Exod 2:1–10) is borrowed from the legendary account of Sargon, the great king of ancient Akkad.

This ancient Mesopotamian king also escaped death as an infant when his mother placed him in a reed basket and floated him down the Euphrates River. Like Moses, he was rescued by a member of a royal household. As a man, Sargon is assisted by the goddess Ishtar to become a great ruler. The core of the story serves the purpose of setting Sargon and Moses aside from their fellows while providing a foundation for the later rise to power. In Moses's case, however, it also means that the hero starts life with one foot in the camp of the oppressed Hebrews and one foot in the palace of the pharaoh. Split between two cultures, forced into exile after an impetuous murder (Exod 2:11–12), and then chosen to return to Egypt as the spokesperson for YHWH (Exod 3:1–4:17), he is portrayed in the narrative as a complex and at times self-doubting individual.

Table 2.2 outlines several of the literary parallels and story elements found in ancient Near Eastern legends and royal inscriptions that also are incorporated into the Moses story.[31]

Moses is such a monumental character that it is difficult to say that individual story elements can capture his full importance to Israelite tradition. His name, generally associated with the events or the exodus, a command from God, or tied to the giving of the law, is constantly referred to by Israelite leaders (Josh 8:31; 14:2), by kings or their scribal chroniclers (1 Kgs 2:3; 8:56; 2 Kgs 23:25), and by the prophets (Isa 63:11–12; Micah 6:4; Mal 4:4). Eventually, the law and Moses become so intertwined that it is difficult to speak of one without the other (2 Chron 35:6; Ezra 3:2; Neh 9:14). Invoking the name of Moses or the "law of Moses" becomes a form of blessing (2 Kgs 21:8) or condemnation (2 Kgs 14:6), depending on whether the event or person described in the text is obedient or in violation of the covenant and its stipulations. Only David will achieve a similar status of authoritative memory as the king whose "heart" was in tune with God's commands (1 Kgs 9:4; 14:8).

Table 2.2

ANCIENT NEAR EASTERN LITERARY PARALLELS TO MOSES NARRATIVE

Precedent	*ANE Parallel*	*Significance*
Miraculous birth narrative (Exod 2:1–10)	Sargon I of Akkad birth narrative (late twenty-fourth-century BCE Mesopotamian king)	Saved from death as an infant and with divine aid brought to supreme leadership role
Forced exile and divine summons to return to lead people (Exod 2:11–4:17)	Idrimi of Alalakh (fifteenth century BCE Syrian ruler)	Life stages from escape to exile and divinely ordered campaign to free people
Marriage and assimilation into pastoral, tribal culture	Sinuhe (nineteenth century BCE; Egyptian story)	Exile marries into family of local chief, lives for many with their tribe
Sequence of plagues (Exod 7:14–12:32)	Atrahasis (seventeenth century BCE; Mesopotamian epic)	Contest between gods includes use of wise human to end plagues
Law giver (Exod 19:20–20:21)	Hammurabi (eighteenth century BCE; Babylonian)	Divinely appointed leader presents laws to the people

CONCLUDING REMARKS

When a conscious effort is made to perpetuate a dynamic collective memory, the past is always immediately present. More than a simple recollection, collective memory functions as an essential aspect of lived reality for a community throughout the years. Should it require a means of preservation or revival, then that conveniently occurs in the form of commemoration, education, recitation, and ritual. Thus, the substance of cherished collective memories, such as the stories of the Israelite ancestors or the exodus event, remain vibrant as long as they continue to be told.

With respect to the ancestors, a close connection is made between them and the covenant promise. The land of promise is always the great prize extended to the people through the covenant (see it denied to the unfaithful in Num 32:11). Thus, in Moses's call to lead the people out of Egypt the deity who addresses him is identified as the "God of your ancestors, the God of Abraham, the God of Isaac, the God of Jacob" (Exod 3:15). That title continues to be used for God throughout Israelite tradition (1 Kgs 18:36; 2 Kgs 13:23).

In the case of the exodus story, it became institutionalized through a divine injunction to teach your children so that they will know that "we were Pharaoh's slaves in Egypt, but the Lord brought us out of Egypt with a mighty hand" (Deut 6:21). By doing so, that story could be retold whenever the people faced oppression from a stronger nation. Egypt also functions as the label for any location from which God will free and restore the captive people (Micah 7:11–15). And, in the end, the admonition to remember Egypt, whenever and for whatever original purpose it was created, becomes a theological survival mechanism for the Israelites for much of their history. It provides a logical theodicy for God's punishment of the people and an ultimate reassurance and incentive that in time they will be liberated and restored to their covenant relationship with all its obligations and benefits.

Given current information, it cannot be said that the ancestral narratives and the exodus story are based on historical events. Their real value is found in how they contribute to the Israelite foundation story. A people without a well-defined identity cannot coalesce into a nation or hope to survive under the pressures of surrounding nations. The ancestral narratives provide the origin story for the establishment of the covenant with God and a host of cultural precedents that will find their way into everyday life and legal tradition. The story of the exodus functions as the "next step" beyond the covenant promise. It celebrates divine intervention on behalf of the covenant community. The contest between gods found in the plague sequence, the demonstration of power over the forces of nature detailed in the Red Sea crossing, and the miraculous military victories in the wilderness provide a picture of God as the supreme creator, who guides and protects the people, but also holds them to a standard of right behavior and belief. That becomes the lesson of the ancestors and the exodus that will be told and retold throughout Israelite history.

3

Settlement and Competition in Iron Age I Canaan

An Archaeological, Political, and Social Perspective

THE FOCUS OF THIS CHAPTER on the Iron I period is twofold. First, we will examine the forces (environmental, economic, and political) that contributed to the nearly complete transformation of the eastern Levant at the end of the Late Bronze Age. Among the topics to be discussed will be the super-power struggles between the Egyptians and the Hittite empire for control of Syria-Palestine that consumed much of their energy during the twelfth century BCE. Of equal importance is the invasion of the region by groups of people collectively referred to as the Sea Peoples. A process of cultural accommodation and reshaping took place over several generations between this Aegean-oriented population and the indigenous Canaanites. Attention also will be given to contacts between the city-states of Philistia as they emerged on Canaan's southern coast, Cyprus, and the Phoenicians in Lebanon. Finally, in this portion of the chapter, attention will be given to the archaeological evidence for the emergence of new settlements in the Central Hill Country of Canaan.

The establishment of these small hilltop village communities and the struggles they faced to make a living off the land will then segue into the other primary focus area. The biblical account of the settlement and "conquest" of Canaan by the Proto-Israelite tribes will be compared to what is known of this time period. I refer to them at this point as "Proto-Israelites" because they have yet to coalesce into an identifiable and united political entity.[1] It will only be possible to speak of them as Israelites after the monarchy is founded and the apparatus of state-building has begun (bureaucracy, organized economic activities, civic works, and a standing military).

During the transition from the Late Bronze Age into the Early Iron Age (thirteenth to eleventh centuries BCE), several marked changes took place in the eastern Levant. The large urban centers of Canaan and Syria that had existed and prospered for at least two centuries had depended on their ability to exploit the natural resources of their region (grain, olive oil, various metals, and luxury goods) and participate in an international trade network that encompassed much of the eastern Mediterranean. Naturally, the super powers in Egypt and Asia Minor (modern Turkey) drew on the wealth and resources of this multifaceted economic activity, while demanding and obtaining tribute from the Syrian seaport city of Ugarit and the other major centers of commerce. Much of this activity was disrupted at the end of the thirteenth century when a variety of factors came together, including climate change (a reduction in annual precipitation between 1250–1100 BCE), frequent warfare, and the incursion of the Sea Peoples. The result will be the destruction of some of these major urban centers (Ugarit) or their decline (Hazor, Megiddo) in importance.

The flourishing international commercial era that helped to enrich palace elites as well as private traders was fragmented, with only portions of the network (i.e., Cyprus to the Phoenician coast) remaining intact.[2] The weakening of the Egyptian and Hittite empires added to the economic uncertainty of the time. However, the need for a resumption of commerce and the exchange of goods helped to energize the efforts of the new peoples from the Aegean area who colonized Cyprus, southern Asia Minor, and the eastern Levantine coast from Lebanon south to Gaza on the Canaanite coast. Egypt did continue to maintain at least limited trade connections with the northern coast of the Levant, especially at Dor and Qasile.[3] Within a generation they will revive the trade networks of the past and expand them during the course of the next two centuries into the western Mediterranean. There is also evidence, based in part on the collection of ivory pieces found at Megiddo and dated to the twelfth century BCE that a short-lived Canaanite political entity existed and prospered as Egyptian control receded.[4]

In order to trace these developments, we need to examine the factors that contributed to the disruption of the political and economic order of the Levant. Where connections can be made between archaeological and lexical data and the biblical account they will be pointed out. However, again, this is a period that does not provide a reliable and verifiable case for the historicity of the biblical narrative. It is possible to discuss such things as the content of written records from Ugarit, Egypt, and the Hittite empire that reflect on commerce, diplomacy, and warfare. There is also a great deal of information on the character of the ceramic assemblage that includes both Canaanite and Helladic types and forms, as well as evidence of efforts to establish new villages in the Central Highlands of Canaan. Actual archaeological data attesting to clashes between the Philistines and Canaanites are less convincing and certainly not systematic. In fact, the names of the new Philistine cities are all Semitic, a curious fact given the Aegean origin of these new colonists, but perhaps a sign of accommodation to new circumstances.

There is some evidence of destruction of city sites during this period that might be ascribed to the emergence of Philistines or to the Proto-Israelites in various areas of Canaan, including the Jezreel Valley, but we have no extrabiblical textual evidence to verify that connection. Instead, what we do have are data indicating (1) the demise or weakening of the super powers in Egypt and Asia Minor (Turkey), and (2) accounts (primarily from Egyptian sources) of invaders collectively referred to as the Sea Peoples, who destabilized the area from Asia Minor to Cyprus to most of Syria-Palestine. Out of this time of social upheaval and with the major players removed or at least diminished in Syria-Palestine, a political vacuum was created that allowed either new peoples to enter the region and/or the amalgamation of a portion of the Canaanites with new groups that eventually form an entirely new set of ethnic groups that will come to dominate the area for the next two centuries.[5]

Thirteenth-Century BCE Geopolitics: Egypt vs. the Hittite Empire

It would be best to begin with a broader picture of the political and economic character of the thirteenth century BCE. For much of that century, pharaoh Ramesses II engaged in both an armed conflict and a sort of "cold war" with the leader of the Hittite empire, Muwatalli II, and his immediate successors. Seeing it as a rich repository of natural resources and an effective, political buffer zone, each major power worked to gain military and diplomatic supremacy over Syria-Palestine and its overland and maritime pathways. Each made use of mercenary troops from the Mediterranean region to enhance their military power. Perhaps the turning point in the international conflict occurred in 1285 BCE at the Battle of Qadesh in northern Syria. While both sides claimed victory, neither was able to advance their territorial claims beyond their previous borders. Furthermore, when a plague broke out among the Hittite troops, possibly due to infection from Egyptian prisoners, the Hittite king became one of its victims. Rather than continue the conflict at that point, a treaty was negotiated between Ramesses II and Hattusili III that marked a stage in their relations in which both sides chose to concentrate on internal matters rather than continue outright conflict.

The Hittite empire in particular was regularly forced to deal with the armed threat from the Kaska tribes in northeastern Asia Minor as well as restive subsidiary allies (vassals) in southern and western Asia Minor. In addition, the rulers of the Middle Assyrian period began to contest with the Hittites for control of what had been the Hurrian kingdom of Mitanni in northern Syria and southeastern Asia Minor. At stake were the passes and trade routes leading into Asia Minor as well as markets in the rich area of Cilicia in southern Asia Minor. When Hittite king Tudhaliya IV failed to defeat Tukulti-Ninurta I (1233–1197 BCE) of Assyria at the battle of Nihriya, it became clear that Hittite control of the routes into Syria and Mesopotamia was lost. Their rulers were able temporarily to stave off other threats, including an assassination attempt, and even for a time, with the help of Ugarit's navy, to gain control of Cyprus.

With an empire already in decline, years of famine coupled with overreliance on the import of grain, and internal dissension among vassals and other members of the royal family, it is not a surprise that the Hittites were vulnerable to the attacks of the Sea Peoples.[6] But in the case of the Hittite empire, many of these northern "Sea Peoples," including the Lukka, the Ekwesh, the Tjeker, and the Denyen, actually have their origin in western and southern Asia Minor.[7] In those regions, food shortages and a shattered economy had driven many people from their villages, taking advantage of a breakdown in the political order. Left unchecked they returned to a piratical existence on land and sea. And, when Suppiluliumas II (1207–1178 BCE) attempted to meet the threat at sea, he forced Ugarit to supply him with a navy, leaving that important port city open to attack and eventual destruction. With no record left by either the Hittites or the rulers of Ugarit describing the final stages of their demise, we must rely on a statement found in the Egyptian pharaoh Ramesses III's inscription at Medinet Habu (ca. 1175 BCE): "no land could stand before their arms." The result for the Hittite realm is a "dark age" marked by decentralized, small settlements in the interior and independent kingdoms along the coast of Asia Minor and the islands immediately off shore.

Egypt's Retrenchment

During the reign of Ramesses II that encompassed much of the thirteenth century BCE a number of administrative posts had been established in the interior of Canaan that gave them firmer control over the trade routes running north into Lebanon and on to Damascus. These "governor's residences" and outposts had provided an administrative network for the Egyptians and helped to control the tribal groups that were disrupting trade and the movement of merchants and royal officials.[8] Both Merneptah (1213–1204 BCE) and Ramesses III (1194–1163 BCE) continued these efforts at taking control of major Canaanite cities along the trade routes (including Ashkelon and Gezer, according to the "Israel Stele" of Merneptah—1208 BCE), and that may have extended their influence as far north as Megiddo in the Jezreel Valley.[9]

However, starting in the eighth year of Ramesses III a retrenchment began as Egyptian forces began a gradual withdrawal from most of Canaan in order to concentrate on Egypt's border defense against the attacks of the Sea Peoples. In essence, by 1135 BCE, Egypt was only able to maintain a presence in the area of Canaan along the coast from Byblos north into Lebanon. By that time, Egyptian "residences" such as those at Lachish and Gezer had been destroyed, marking the political change that had come to the region.[10]

Unfortunately, there is little documentation of the events outlined above. Egyptian sources include the records and inscriptions of Ramesses III and Ramesses IV. They describe how Egypt "defeated" the various elements of the Sea Peoples, which basically means that they were unsuccessful in their efforts to invade and conquer Egypt. But these records, coupled with archaeological evidence, also indicate that Egyptian hegemony over Canaan was either broken or badly damaged. Curiously, no records of these events have been recovered from Philistine sites, despite a great deal of effort over the past forty years. With no accounts available for the demise of the Hittite empire or Ugarit, we are forced to rely on the archaeological evidence of the fiery destruction of their cities to tell that tale.

While some inland Canaanite cities in the Shephelah plateau, like Beth-shemesh, were able to resist Philistine incursions, many others contributed to the number of displaced refugees who fled into the central highland area. That left most of the coastal plain, the sea coast cities of Acco and Dor, and the western Shephelah plateau to the Philistines.[11] The newly installed population with its cultural roots in the Mediterranean region established five city-states (Gaza, Ashkelon, Ashdod, Gath, and Ekron) and became the dominant political presence throughout the rest of the twelfth and eleventh centuries BCE.

The Sea Peoples' Invasion of the Levant

During what archaeologists refer to as the transition from the Late Bronze Age into the Early Iron Age, much of the twelfth century BCE was characterized by the multipronged invasion of the Sea Peoples and its aftermath. Most important for the later history of Israel, these invaders weakened Egyptian and Hittite claims to Syria-Palestine. In addition, they captured and destroyed the influential seaport city of Ugarit on Syria's northern coast, temporarily destabilizing international trade until new Canaanite commercial centers at Tyre and Sidon reestablished these important economic links and trading relationships. To the north and east, the various groups collectively referred to as the Sea Peoples added to the ongoing destabilization of the Hittite empire in Asia Minor that had begun with a major shift in the climate in the Levant during the mid-thirteenth century BCE and extending to 1100 BCE.[12] In western Asia Minor, this ecological crisis had led to famine and the migration of whole populations out of the affected areas, as well as heightened political instability. Eventually, under pressure from these invaders and traditional political enemies the Hittite empire basically ceased to exist, with its capital at Hattusa abandoned even before attackers put its monumental buildings to the torch.[13]

Adding to the mounting power vacuum during this period, no new super power was able to emerge from Mesopotamia during the next two centuries. That lack of centralized administration by a major power allowed Cyprus, Cilicia in southern Asia Minor, and much of the coastal region of Syria and Lebanon to coalesce into new political units by the tenth century BCE. They were settled in many cases by a combination of indigenous inhabitants and the descendants of the Sea Peoples. Ultimately, Ugarit's demise and a lack of control by the Egyptians created an opportunity for the undamaged Phoenician ports of Tyre and Sidon, which were located further south along the coast, but within easy reach of Cyprus. Their continued access to local sources of lumber, purple dye, and olive oil allowed them to prosper and eventually to dominate the maritime trade, especially with Cyrus and the Aegean world.[14] While there apparently was a brief hiatus in the larger network of economic activity in the eastern Levant during the transition from Late Bronze to Early Iron, within a period of a century it had resumed and grown to extend well into the western Mediterranean.

Reshaping of Canaan: Philistines

As the thirteenth century BCE drew to its end, the Levant experienced a period of political and social transformation that had major repercussions throughout Canaan and its neighboring areas. Of particular importance for our understanding of the biblical account of the history of ancient Israel, this is the period that is associated in the narrative with the settlement and "conquest" of Canaan. As part of our discussion in this portion of the chapter we will examine the cultural entanglement process that took place during Iron I (twelfth to eleventh centuries BCE) in which portions of the Late Bronze Canaanite population initially mixed with the colonizing Philistine groups along the coastal plain and later in the Shephelah.

Many of the Canaanite settlements in the Shephelah plateau and adjoining hill country that had functioned as part of a "symbiotic" economic system during the Late Middle Bronze period were destroyed or abandoned in Early Iron I. The displaced people from these settlements may have initially turned to a seminomadic, pastoral existence.[15] Eventually, however, many returned to a sedentary life in the newly established villages in the Central Hill Country. There without the political and economic interference of Egyptian or Canaanite authorities, they may have mixed with newly arrived tribal peoples, possibly including the Proto-Israelites, remnants of the Hittite empire, and others we have yet to identify.[16]

Two pieces of evidence are connected with the appearance of new people in the southern coastal area of Canaan. First is the drop in the total number of settlements and a concentration of the population in the five pentapolis cities associated with the Philistines (Gaza, Ashkelon, Ashdod, Tel Miqne/

Ekron, and Tell es-Ṣafi/Gath.[17] There is evidence at some of these sites (Ekron and Ashdod) of a destruction layer immediately preceding Philistine construction.[18] However, it is not clear that the entrance of these representatives of the Sea Peoples was generally violent, despite the reference to the displacement of the people of Gaza by the Capthorim (Cretans) in Deut 2:23. The archaeological record suggests that the indigenous peoples of Canaan and these migrants may have quickly accommodated to each other's presence and shared their space while maintaining some aspects of their original culture.[19] As such, it is inappropriate to describe the process of Philistine settlement in Canaan as a simple or even predatory colonialization of the area.

The second piece of evidence placing the Philistines in Canaan during the twelfth century BCE is found in the Egyptian Onomasticon of Amenope. The inscription contains a list of place-names coupled with a list of peoples. In this case, the names of three of the Philistine pentapolis cities (Ashkelon, Ashdod, and Gaza) are paired with the names of three of the groups associated with the Sea Peoples: Sherden, Tjeker/Sikel, and the Peleset.[20] The Onomasticon serves as an official record of the political divisions in that area of Canaan and verifies the existence of the Philistine pentapolis at least by 1100 BCE.

After establishing themselves, however, there are indications in the archaeological record that the relationship between the indigenous Canaanite population and the new arrivals was not based entirely on a form of colonial primacy or hostility. Analysis of ceramic remains from the early Iron I has shown that while their pottery styles are distinct, representing different cultures, all of the houses that have been excavated in the Philistine Pentapolis cities have nearly equal quantities of Philistine and Canaanite pottery types.[21] To be sure, these Aegean-based migrants initially held on to some of their cultural associations with the past. For instance, certain ceramic patterns and shapes as well as "symposium-like" feasting rituals are clearly associated with their Aegean heritage.[22] But it is impossible to definitively determine whether these ceramic forms and ritual practices were based on cultural nostalgia or commemoration or served as an effort to draw strict cultural boundary markers between themselves and the Canaanite population.

Given the conclusion that these migrants did settle in Canaan after 1200 BCE, the question that then arises is who are the Philistines and where did they come from? Are they a single ethnic group associated with the Sea Peoples or are they made up of several different peoples? If their number consists of a combination of different peoples, some from the Aegean world and some from the migrating population of southern Asia Minor, what shared objective brought them to southern Canaan to find a new place to settle? And did they all arrive by sea or did some enter Canaan by an overland route?

Determining the ethnic identity of the Philistines or any other group of people based on a list of traits, including distinctive artifacts, forms of technology, clothing, ritual performance, language, and dietary preferences[23] cannot provide a complete picture.[24] It may be enough here to say that the elements of the Sea Peoples, who will eventually be identified collectively as Philistines, probably represent several different groups of people. Some of their cultural traits can be identified with those in the Aegean area, but through a process of entanglement and negotiation, some elements may also have come from the indigenous Canaanite culture.[25]

Ultimately, their social identity as Philistines would have been formed after they entered Canaan. As migrants to a new area, it would have been necessary to be strategic as they negotiated among themselves and with the indigenous population to determine what best contributed to their survival and assimilation to their new home.[26] When identifiable social customs, such as a particular form of feasting, were retained, that may be seen as a form of "boundary marker" deemed necessary to retain and commemorate or to reinforce a portion of their heritage, and as a factor in differentiating themselves from other groups. Similarly, when a customary behavior or practice disappeared, that may serve as evidence either that it was no longer considered essential as a boundary marker or that it eventually was considered to be counter to a peaceful or accommodating association with the people around them. Given time, the process resulted in the development of sufficient, specific cultural characteristics so that the people themselves and their neighbors could identify them as an identifiable and distinctive ethnic group.[27]

Given the relatively small carrying capacity of Late Bronze Age sailing vessels, it seems unlikely that the Philistines came exclusively by sea, but their knowledge of Canaan could have come from previous experience as Egyptian mercenary troops or as maritime traders. That could have helped them to decide where to settle. In addition, large groups of migrants could have made the trek from southern Asia Minor without too much interference after the disintegration of the Hittite empire and the destruction of Ugarit by following the coastal highway.[28]

To this point scholars have attempted to identify "Philistine" artifacts based on ceramic styles of decoration (monochrome or bichrome) and function (kraters, cooking pots, and bell-shaped bowls). However, the full assemblage of pottery found at Philistine sites also includes typical Canaanite storage jars and other everyday common ware. That suggests that these Philistine households may have retained some specific pottery types for table service or cultic practice while adopting Canaanite pottery for other usage.[29]

Additional diagnostic items include the preference for rectangular, plastered cooking hearths (both indoor and outdoor at various sites), spool-shaped loom weights, and some dietary preferences (pork). Modifications in Late Bronze Canaanite architecture also indicate the introduction of new floor plans, cooking areas, and a cottage weaving industry.[30] Arguments have been made for the identification of Philistine sites based on the relative count of pig bones. However, a predilection for pork consumption has come into question by some scholars. They point to ecological conditions (some areas are more suited to raising pigs than others) and suggest this may not be an effective ethnic marker.[31]

Based on the Aegean styles of their pottery, it does seems clear that elements of the Philistines came from or were familiar with the Mycenaean culture of Bronze Age Greece, but there is also evidence of influences from Minoan and Cypriot cultural styles and cultic practices. For example, the "cult corners" and notched scapulae found at various sites, especially in combination with olive oil or textile production or metal working, suggest ties to Cypriot "sacred economy," tying production to the invocation of the gods.[32] There are some new technologies introduced in the Early Iron I period that may also be associated with this new population. They include Aegean-style, hydraulic plastered hearths and floors, new forms of pottery manufacture, and new techniques in weaving.[33] The fact that their creation and use of seals for administrative purposes tends to be more akin to the Aegean practice again points to the mixture of cultural backgrounds among the Philistine settlers.[34]

Finally, there is textual evidence that these people, who will eventually coalesce into the Philistines, spoke several different languages. Unfortunately, it has not yet been possible to decipher their written language from the small number of inscriptions discovered to date, although it seems to have connections to Cypro-Minoan script, Luwian (southern Asia Minor), and Mycenaean Greek. The complexity of languages would be typical of a mixed population of migrants, who may have included scribes fleeing the destruction of their homes in the Aegean area. When a knowledge of neighboring languages became more of a necessity after the Philistine city-states were well established in Iron II, it appears that they adopted the Phoenician and Proto-Hebraic script, but the people may well have continued to speak variants of their original languages.[35]

Reshaping of Canaan: Proto-Israelites

Turning to another area of Canaan during the twelfth century BCE, archaeological excavations and surveys have provided a fairly exact picture of the emergence of new settlement patterns in the Central Highlands.[36] This pattern contrasts with the abandonment of many of the villages in the Shephelah during Iron I, leaving only a small enclave of Canaanite settlements in the eastern portion of that region.[37] In the Central Highlands, however, hundreds of new village sites began to be constructed that generally housed approximately 100 to 150 persons, with a total approximate population of 55,000.[38] These small settlements were located sufficiently inland, ranging from Jerusalem north to the Jezreel Valley.[39] They were isolated enough that they were not considered to be a political or military threat by the Philistines or other inhabitants of the lowlands and coastal region. Set in an area previously underpopulated because of the environmental challenges involved there, they were left to scratch out an existence from the meager resources provided by that region.

Forced to manage with such a small population, these villages would have had to rely on the individual abilities of each member of the community. One way of describing such an interdependent society is as a heterarchy. This social classification takes into account that rank within a group may vary depending on the task at hand and does not fall into a binary classification (elite vs. nonelite) that is inherent to hierarchical systems.[40] In a heterarchy, every able-bodied person of both genders would have worked in the fields, managed the small herds, and performed the everyday domestic and maintenance tasks associated with their dwellings and small cottage industries. When leadership or expertise was required to perform a particular task, then the best person for that role would step forward or be identified by the group. Thus the variability of leadership would be the primary characteristic of these small communities. In this way they had a better chance to survive and produce sufficient food to stave off the exigencies of periodic famine and attendant malnutrition.[41] It is even possible that the lack of evidence for Iron I burials associated with these villages is due to the general poverty of the villagers and the simple lack of time to devote to carving out elaborate burial chambers or caves.[42]

The Central Highlands was indeed an environmentally challenging area despite the fact that pollen studies have shown that by the end of the twelfth century BCE the average rainfall had once again increased to normal levels.[43] Following a pattern that occurred during the Middle Bronze I period when the climate once again became wetter, the "greening" of previously dry areas would have enticed peoples from the steppes to move into fertile valleys as well as new areas such as the Central Highlands.[44]

Even with more predictable rainfall amounts, the basic character of a Mediterranean climate means that yearly rainfall is limited to the fall and early winter (October to February). Given that climatic reality, settlements would have gravitated to locations near perennial springs and would have had to learn dry-farming techniques.[45] Many of the hillsides already had been badly eroded in antiquity due to earlier deforestation. Agricultural activity that did not attempt to prevent further erosion would have required the settlers to move periodically to a new location. Most of the arable, flat land was found in mountainous valleys that also served as the principal pathways from the hill country back to the Shephelah. That meant that areas containing considerable amounts of arable land like the Elah Valley were often in dispute (see the setting for the story of Goliath and the Philistine threat to Saul's army in 1 Sam 17:1–3).

These conditions required the new inhabitants, whether they were displaced Canaanites, newly arrived pastoral nomadic tribes or others, to develop or borrow from their neighbors' innovative solutions to increase their harvests and to introduce crops and other agricultural produce that could thrive there. Agricultural surveys have produced ceramic remains, including large pithoi jars for storage or grain or water as well as flint sickle blades that echo past harvests. Given the conditions, the villagers in this region came to depend on the planting and cultivation of cereal grains, olives, and grapes.[46]

Quite simply, even on the small scale needed to sustain a village, they had to learn from and adapt to their new environment. For example, it would not be possible to plow their fields during dry months when the ground would be sun-hardened from lack of rain. Plowing with a team of oxen (1 Sam 11:5) could only occur with the coming of the winter rains (Prov 20:4). When sufficient moisture loosened up the soil, the diligent villagers could resume the agricultural cycle, plowing first to break up the ground and to arrest the growth of weeds, and then plowing a second time to facilitate the sowing of the seed.[47]

The construction of terraces on the slopes of badly eroded hillsides near their settlements, while not necessarily a new innovation, became another key to survival for the highland villages.[48] Building terraces did not become a pervasive or systematic practice until the Iron II period when the population grew larger. Still, it placed great strain on the people to erect and maintain them (see Isa 5:1–7).[49] The heavy workload of transporting soil to fill the terraces necessitated cooperation by the entire community. Working together as a social unit also built strong affiliations and contributed to the development of a new social identity. Eventually, they would be able to see themselves as no longer just the remnants of Canaanite refugees, migrants from other parts of the Levant, or tribal groups coming out of the desert and steppe regions of the Sinai and Midian (Deut 1:6–3:29). Within this social cauldron they could freely mix their cultures and their households to become the Proto-Israelites, who eventually would form the core of an emerging ethnic group during the formation of larger chiefdoms by Saul and David in the tenth century BCE.

Much of the story of these pioneers is based around the social adjustments that small communities must make as they work in unison for their mutual benefit as equals. Under these conditions, there could be no discrimination based on age, gender or previous cultural background when it took the efforts of all the people simply to produce enough food to survive, especially in an environment regularly subject to drought and famine (Deut 28:22). It is not surprising therefore that the biblical narratives that are set in the time period of the settlement focused on the lives of villagers, including their efforts to farm and manage small herds of sheep and goats, and their struggles to maintain themselves in the face of environmental and physical threats from their neighbors (Judg 6:3–6).

Using the Settlement Narrative

Because of the complex nature of their composition and the Deuteronomistic editing of the materials found in the books of Deuteronomy, Joshua, Judges, and 1 Samuel, they cannot be used indiscriminately as a source for the reconstruction of the history of the Iron I period. Still, it is likely that the seventh-century BCE Deuteronomistic Historian at least in part pieced together a version of Israelite history using extant court records and long-preserved oral traditions.[50] And, in fact, these narratives do contain fragments of ancient songs ("Song of Deborah"—Judg 5), legendary stories of heroes (Joshua, Shamgar, Gideon, Samson), and the origin story for the emergence of a chiefdom out of the disorganized, temporary tribal alliances described in the Book of Judges. Holding the narratives together, however, is an editorially imposed, theological foundation designed to make the case for (1) YHWH's willingness to provide the Israelites with a path to redemption if they return to full compliance with the covenant (Judg 2:11–23), and (2) a rationale for the creation of the Israelite monarchy. Thus the reiteration of the phrase "In those days there was no king in the land" (Judg 18:1a; 19:1a; 21:25) signals a contrast by the Deuteronomist between the political chaos of the Judges period and the proffered order once the monarchy is established.

Even within these shaped traditions, the narratives do provide useful information on the conditions in the premonarchic village culture that can be helpful to our reconstruction when coupled with the archaeological data that have emerged from excavations and surveys of the ancient sites in the Central Highlands. There are allusions to ancient farming methods, herding, village politics, family relations, and religious practices. Of course, there are also stories dealing with the interaction between the Proto-Israelite villagers, the Philistines, and other peoples of Canaan and Transjordan. While they tell us little about actual historical events, these narratives are worth examining, especially in terms of the development of cultural boundary markers by the various peoples in the Central Highlands as they began to merge into a people eventually identified as the Israelites. In addition, the nearly three hundred references to the Philistines in these texts are a further testament to ancient Israel's efforts to define itself over and against an "enemy," who is determined to be different from them in so many ways.

Biblical References to the Philistines

Nations often characterize themselves by saying what they are and what they are not. For example, one simple way that the Israelites vilified and contrasted themselves with the Philistines was to refer to them as the "uncircumcised" (Judg 14:3; 15:18). The biblical narrative spends a great deal of time framing Israel in terms of its religious practices, its commitment to the covenant with YHWH, and its legal pronouncements. However, there is also a real sense in the text of the "culture war" championed by the Deuteronomist in which the Israelites are repeatedly warned to avoid adopting or adapting to the religious practices of their neighbors (see Deut 30:11–20; Judg 2:1–5). To be able to identify these forbidden practices, the Israelite storytellers and scribes would, by necessity, have had to know something about them. And, the military, economic, and social contacts with the neighboring peoples, including the Philistines, would have provided that knowledge.

As is so often the case in the biblical narrative, however, the normal interaction between peoples becomes the basis for conflict. For example, Samson's desire to marry a Philistine woman despite the concerns of his parents seems on its face to be an expected result of two peoples living in close proximity (Judg 14:1–3). However, the Deuteronomist inserts a "footnote" in the text to indicate that the match is part of a divine plan to bring Samson's remarkable strength to bear on the Philistines (Judg 14:4). Thus begins a competition between cultures that results in the destruction of property (Judg 15:3–5) and the deaths of thousands (Judg 15:15–16; 16:28–30). Conflicts happen, of course, but the point made in the biblical account is that they occur or are staged in order to protect the Israelites from assimilation with noncovenantal people.

As noted above, the Philistines are unlikely to have been a single people when they first migrated or settled in Canaan.

Their mixed cultural heritage did eventually begin to amalgamate into a more cohesive and identifiable group characterized by the appearance of local cultural features and Phoenician influences by the Iron IIA period in the ninth century BCE.[51] The fact that they never combined into a single nation and were associated instead with a loosely allied pentapolis of city-states (Judg 3:3) suggests that they chose to cooperate when not openly competing with each other.[52] However, they never merged into a single political entity.

There is even the possibility that at times during the Israelite monarchy period that a Philistine city would side with Judah against another Philistine city.[53] Their failure to unite eventually caused them difficulties later when the Assyrians invaded the region in the late eighth century BCE (Sargon II's campaign in 711 BCE; Isa 20:1; Amos 1:6–8). During the period of the settlement in the eleventh to tenth centuries, however, the Philistines would have been a real obstacle to the loosely affiliated tribes and chieftains of the Proto-Israelites, who occupied the Central Highlands.

References in the biblical text indicate that the Philistine economy prospered within the richer and better watered lands along the coast, growing wheat (Judg 15:1) and cultivating olive orchards (Judg 15:5) and growing grapes (Judg 14:5).[54] Naturally, the Philistines' success in establishing themselves along the coastal plain and on the fringes of the western Shephelah (Josh 13:2–3) made them a natural competitor for the peoples settled within the less fertile Central Highlands. As such, in an era when the Proto-Israelites were finding ways to survive in the highlands they quickly discovered that they would be unable to expand into the richer lands to the north and west unless they found a way to compete with the technologically and politically more sophisticated Canaanite and Philistine cities. That ultimately meant that they had to evolve politically from an "inchoate state," marked by allegiance based on kinship ties and identification with a defined tribal or community territory into an "early state," whose leadership was open to using officials not dependent on kinship affiliations. In this way they would have a better chance to expand both physically and conceptually beyond their original territorial boundaries and occupy larger regions as a cohesive political entity.[55]

These Proto-Israelites were faced with two primary problems beyond the rather sparse environmental resources in the highlands. They could have easily seen the richer areas to the west and especially in the Shephelah, but they were constrained from possessing them since conflict with the coastal cities was beyond their ability. And in any case they needed to maintain the trade exchanges that helped both economies (generally involving exchange of woolen goods and olive oil for grain and manufactured goods). It should be noted that the geographical character of the Shephelah, which rose gradually from the coastal plain and served as both a buffer zone and a conduit for travel between the coast and the highlands, did have a major effect on relations between the Philistine and Canaanite city-states and the village culture in the high country.

Within an area of approximately twenty-eight miles running north to south and just over nine miles wide, there existed several east-west valleys with the Shephelah that connected the coast with the highlands, potentially promoting trade and the transport of goods and commodities and facilitating the movement of armies.[56] Of course, there were some settlements in the Shephelah, most prominent of which were the fortified cities of Timnah and Beth-shemesh.[57] Excavations have shown that these towns had contact with both Philistine and Proto-Israelite cultures, and in later periods they passed politically and economically back and forth between these two competing peoples (2 Chron 26:6–10; 28:18).

The other problem that ultimately became a motivation to do more than simply accept their lot in the highlands was the physical reality of spatial circumscription, a condition in which a people have outgrown the resources of the area in which they live. As a result they were increasingly handicapped in their efforts to support their growing population and, at the same time, were restrained from expanding beyond their territory without coming into conflict with their neighbors. Their ability to engage in trade was also at risk if the coastal cities became concerned with raids and banditry (Judg 5:6–7; 11:3) and chose to cut them off by force if necessary (1 Sam 13:17–18).

Signs of the real and potential tension or competition between these people are found in the biblical text in respect to certain types of technology such as metalworking. The lack of artifactual evidence calls into doubt that the Philistines actually had a large scale, iron-based technology during the early Iron I period.[58] Still, the reference in 1 Sam 13:19–21, however exaggerated it may be, is an indication that the Proto-Israelites were not as sophisticated in working metal as the Philistines. After all, living in the highlands, the Proto-Israelites would not have direct access to the sources of either copper or iron and would be less equipped to work these metals.[59]

Furthermore, other references to iron in the biblical narrative, including the "iron chariots" in Judg 1:19 and Goliath's array of armament that includes a spearhead weighing "six hundred shekels of iron" (1 Sam 17:5–7), support the "underdog" motif of the Proto-Israelites. They gain their military victories through their collaboration with YHWH, the divine warrior, rather than their technological skills. In addition, the peoples of Canaan during the settlement period continued to depend largely on bronze implements and weapons. That, in turn, means that a well-trained smith would have been prized by either culture in that or later periods (2 Kgs 24:14, 16).

In some cases the inability of the Proto-Israelites to compete with their more advanced neighbors meant having to find an alternative to staying in one place. For example, the tribe of Dan is said to have migrated away from their original allotment since it was in close proximity to Philistine territory (Josh 19:40–46). It is possible that the difficulties between the Proto-Israelite tribes, including Dan and Judah, as well as the Philistines that are described in the Samson narratives (see esp. Judg 15:9–11), are a further indication that migration was a viable option. Interestingly, the opportunistic character of the Danites is implicit when they relocate into the northern Galilee region and establish themselves at Laish/Leshem, which they then rename the city of Dan (Josh 19:47–48; Judg 18:27–31). That also points to the fluid nature of the settlement period when groups of people shifted about until they could create a stronghold that they could defend and in which they could prosper.

Ultimately, what would be needed for the highland villagers who choose to stay in Canaan was to find a way to cooperate in order to gain military and economic parity with the peoples who were holding them in check. In some respects that also included developing an ideology identifying their western competitors as "greedy" or "unclean" (i.e., uncircumcised) or the worshippers of false gods. An expression of an anti-Canaanite polemic in the Song of Deborah in Judges 5, which is set in the area of the Jezreel Valley, begins with a hymn to YHWH's power and might (5:1–5), then vilifies the wealthy who oppress the "peasantry of Israel" (5:10), followed by a blessing of the faithful tribes and a shaming of those who stayed at home in the crisis (5:14–18). The song concludes with the miraculous victory of the Israelite tribes with YHWH's help (5:19–23), the glorification of Deborah and Yael for their courage against the enemy (5:24–27), and a comic reversal, turning Sisera's mother's expectation of loot into ashes (5:28–30). By using various forms of propaganda, the highlanders were able to transform their foes into villains fated to perish at the hands of YHWH's "friends" (5:31).

Life in the Highland Villages

Based on an analysis of survey and archaeological data over the past thirty years, it is possible to demonstrate that there were hundreds of new highland villages that were established during the Iron I period, but they were quite small and scattered along the ridges of the hills and in narrow mountain valleys. It also can be assumed that life in the highlands was rather harsh and filled with the work necessary for simple survival. Examination of animal bones from these villages has established that the people had a mixed economy of agriculture combined with the management of sheep, goats, and cattle (Judg 6:4). Kinship relations and a shared purpose in a marginal environment would have held them together, but it is doubtful that during the early Iron Age these small communities had much time to devote to matters other than their work in the fields of wheat and barley, the cultivation of their olive groves and grape vines, and the management of their flocks of sheep and goats. Examination of the faunal remains from these villages also show that they relied on donkeys for transportation (Josh 15:18; Judg 19:28), and these sturdy animals gave them the ability to carry heavy loads, including the large collared-rim jars that helped them transport water to their terraced fields.[60]

As outlined in the tenth-century BCE Gezer Calendar and references in the biblical narratives, the village year revolved around the agricultural seasons from planting to harvesting to feasting. The entire village would have turned out to harvest the fields using flint sickle blades embedded in wooden handles (Deut 16:9). The harvested stalks of grain were brought to a centrally located, communal threshing floor (Deut 16:13; Job 5:26; Micah 4:12). A threshing sledge was pulled by oxen over the piles of grain to break them up and to assist with removing the chaff from the kernels of wheat (2 Sam 24:22). This was followed by a winnowing (Ruth 3:2) and sieving process (Sir

27:4) that eventually resulted in piles of grain free of debris and arranged around the floor of the facility (Ruth 3:3). In a similar way, when the sheep were brought together for shearing (Gen 38:13; 1 Sam 25:2), that phase of the herding process was completed, bills were paid, and all debts from the previous year were reconciled.

At that point, the threshing floor or the place of shearing took on another, enhanced social characteristic. Instead of just being a communal place for the work of processing grain, it became a place associated with the future plans of the community, embodied in the distribution of the grain or the fleeces of sheared sheep.[61] Of course, because they were gathering places and sources of loot, the threshing floor and the village storage silos also became a focal point for raiders, who wished to steal or destroy the harvest (Judg 6:3–5).

When it became necessary to make decisions that affected the entire village, a group of elders would assemble either at the threshing floor or at the entrance to the village (Deut 21:19; 22:15) and form a consensus on what needed to be done for the benefit of the community. The location is significant because of the continual traffic to or through these places, making them natural locations for the gathering of the elders. In later periods, it may have become a scribal convention to refer to gatherings of elders or judges in the gate, even when that was more of a euphemism for the entrance into a village rather than a reference to settlements that were protected by a wall system (Ruth 4:1–6). While there is no law in the biblical text that states that the elders were required to spend their time sitting in the gate in case someone would appear to seek a decision on a civil matter, it is likely that they may have often chosen to sit in the gate because it was a place to transact business, to share gossip, and to demonstrate their status as men of property and influence (see Lot's station in Gen 19:1 and the well-respected man who is "known in the city gates" in Prov 31:23).

Village-Based Religious Practices

Despite the description of the appointment of Aaron and his descendants as priests over the Israelites (Exod 28:1; 29:4–9) as well as the detailing of the duties assigned to the Levites during the exodus and wilderness narratives (Exod 38:21; Num 1:50–51; 3:1–13), the reality is that the portrayal of the village culture in the Book of Judges contains very few references to the Levites or to organized cultic procedures being directed by Levites. Instead these Proto-Israelite villagers, collectively, and within their small communities and households had to be fairly self-reliant when it came to making sacrifices or engaging in other cultic activities that in later periods will be associated with the Levitical priests and the temple community.

It is possible that the lack of Levites may simply be a part of the overall Deuteronomic portrayal in Judges of a period of social chaos, civil war, and violations of traditional practices. More likely, however, the very small number of Levites mentioned in these stories reflects the conditions of a rural culture in general. They neither needed someone dedicated solely to cultic activity nor could they afford to support him and his family. It is possible, however, that some Levites did take on the role of mediator between the various tribal leaders and in that way facilitated the eventual transition to chiefdoms and a more unified community.[62]

Given the absence of Levites or of a priestly community in the Judges narrative, the normal cultic practices that composed "family religion" appear to be placed in the hands of the head of household rather than a trained priest just as it was in the ancestral narratives (see Gen 12:7–8).[63] Thus ritual actions such as those described in Exod 12:1–3, 8–11, and 21–23 would have been conducted by the head of household, not by priests or Levites.[64] For example, in several cases when sacrificial altars are mentioned, they seem to be erected as part of an ad hoc process designed to commemorate a theophany (Judg 6:24) or to entreat God to help them deal with a current dilemma (Judg 21:3–4). The ability to erect an altar wherever convenient is also found in the story of Samson's father Manoah, who takes advantage of a convenient rock formation on his family's property that could serve as a makeshift platform for his offering to the Lord rather than going to a standard cultic site (Judg 13:15–20).[65]

In the only explicit instance in which the Judges narrative mentions an established, working altar in an Israelite village, it is dedicated to the Canaanite god Ba'al rather than to YHWH (Judg 6:25). Its presence speaks to a time when a mixed population and a culture that had not yet formed explicit religious boundaries or allegiances lived on the edge of survival. The people may have seen an advantage in combining the worship of various gods in order to obtain divine assistance. So wedded are the villagers of Ophrah to this sacred site with its altar and Asherah pole (6:25) that it requires the intervention of a very reluctant Gideon, at God's command, to tear it down and then erect an altar on a high place suitable for sacrifices to YHWH (6:26–27). Even then, Gideon fears a violent reaction by the villagers at the loss of their Ba'al altar since religious practices tend to be very conservative and difficult to change once a pattern has been set. It takes his father, who had originally build the altar to this local god, to save the day by challenging Ba'al to defend his altar if he can (6:29–31). In no case, however, is a Levite priest mentioned as ministering before this village altar or any other. The lack of specialization within the village context fits well with what we know of the hill country villages.

Transition from Inchoate to Early State

Limited to primarily legendary materials available to us in the books of Joshua and Judges and the early chapters of 1 Samuel, it is difficult to paint a totally accurate picture of the political character of the highland settlements during the Iron I period. While some of these stories or elements of the stories may contain fragments from earlier oral traditions and reports of actual events, they have been edited into a narrative fabric with its own purposes. In some cases, that means that stories are included or re-shaped to fit theological, ideological, or political purposes that reflect a later time period in Israel's history. Using caution, we can draw on some of these details to help reconstruct life and social institutions, but as was the case in our discussion of the ancestral narratives, we need to recognize that biblical history writing and modern history writing are not the same thing.[66]

While it is best to recognize that the biblical narratives are a reflection of the cultural forces that were influencing the author(s) and the audience at the time of composition/editing,[67] that does not discount the possibility that they also contain fragments of traditions and memories of life in the Iron I period. For instance, there are numerous references to geographic areas, cities, and natural phenomena (caves, springs, landmarks). Some of these places have been identified, but the question remains of whether these references contain data associated with the Iron I period or a later time period. Since there are no references to known rulers in these materials from Deuteronomy through Judges, we should suspend judgment on the historicity of the events described. It is also possible that their absence reflects a time of political flux when the major powers in Egypt and Mesopotamia are not actively engaged in Canaan, and history is therefore local.

Geography: Place-Names and the Significance of Places

There are a number of population centers mentioned in the biblical narratives, but it is important to keep in mind that history does not just happen in cities. During the Iron I period and even the Iron II period a large proportion of the settlers in the hill country, extending south to Beer-sheba, lived in small villages that may have had a short lifespan and thus left little if any trace for archaeologists.[68] Cities during that period housed elites and functioned as administrative, manufacturing, and distribution centers and therefore would have left more evidence to be examined by archaeologists. However, some of the cities that are listed as being destroyed by the Israelites during their conquest of Canaan, including Arad (Num 21:1–3), Hebron (Josh 10:36–37), and Ai (Josh 8:1–29), were not occupied during the Late Bronze Age, and in fact some were abandoned ruins throughout much of the second millennium BCE.[69] The capture of Jericho and Hazor forms a major part of the conquest itinerary in Joshua 1–12, but the archaeological record does not contain destruction levels during the twelfth century that correspond with this account.

In addition, the "holy war" (*ḥerem*) context of the Joshua conquest account removes many of the normal military aspects of an invasion force that would ordinarily focus on siege tactics and looting of conquered cities. Instead it replaces these practices with ritual behavior (the seven-fold encompassing procession around Jericho—Josh 6) or with accounts of divine intervention (the "sun stands still" at Gibeon—Josh 10:12–13). The theological emphasis applied to these stories fits better into the seventh-century fervor of Josiah's reform movement. It provides an underpinning for the restoration of YHWH worship as directed by the "Book of the Law" and Josiah's proclaimed efforts to cleanse the temple and the nation of false doctrine. The stories also fit into a common practice in the ancient Near East of manipulating narratives for political or propagandistic purposes.[70]

That calculated usage of traditions in turn can be coupled with the admonitions in the biblical text to engage in "ethnic cleansing" (Deut 7:1–6; Josh 7:10; 17:17–18). However, this ideology, with its charge to eliminate the Canaanite population as a means of removing temptation from the Israelites to assimilate or to engage in cultural borrowing, has more to do with later Israelite history than with this earlier era when there were so many displaced people. A similar elimination of indigenous populations in the Transjordanian trek (Deut 2:26–3:7) seems predicated simply on taking nonhuman booty and clearing the land of competitors while leaving it open for Israelite settlement.[71]

In some cases, sites mentioned in either the Joshua account (Gibeon—el-Jib, 5.6 miles north of Jerusalem) or the episodes in Judges (Gibeah—Tell el-Ful, 3.4 miles north of Jerusalem; Judg 19) were known to be functioning settlements in the eleventh to tenth centuries BCE.[72] However, it is more important to note that these sites also functioned as part of a fairly transparent political polemic associated with the political ideology of the eighth or seventh century BCE rather than the Iron I period. Archaeological investigation has shown that Gibeon, Saul's home city, functioned as a cultic center before the reign of Solomon (see its association with Solomon in 1 Kgs 3:4–9 and his subsequent transferral of religious supremacy to Jerusalem in 3:15).[73] If it remained as a major religious center in the later monarchy period, Gibeon would therefore have been a prime target of Josiah's centralizing reform as he attempted to close local religious sites and elevate Jerusalem as Judah's cultic center (2 Kgs 23:8). It is possible therefore that the ruse perpetrated on Joshua by the Gibeonites and their craven attempts to save themselves at the expense of the Canaanite kings (Josh 9:3–15; 10:6) serves as a form of propaganda designed to justify the removal of their cultic designation as a recognized Israelite worship site.[74]

Similarly, in the late settlement period, Gibeah, a city in the tribal territory of Benjamin, is identified as Saul's capital city (1 Sam 10:26) and the seat of his administration after being recognized as the leader of the Israelite tribes (1 Sam 22:6). However, it also is highlighted in the Judges narrative as the site of one of the most despicable crimes in the settlement period and the focal point of a civil war between the tribes (Judg 19:12–30; 20:8–11). By combining the shameful act perpetrated at Gibeah in the Judges account with Saul's tribal and family associations with this site, the biblical writer may have been attempting to further the political aim of disqualifying the Saulide clan from any future claim to the kingship and legitimizing the House of David.[75] It is also possible that the political "triangle" found in the story of Bethlehem (David's city), Ephraim (the principal northern tribe), and Gibeah of Saul may also be a representation of the tensions that led to the division of the kingdom after Solomon's death.[76]

Material Culture and History

In an earlier section of this chapter we explored the artifactual remains that helped to identify the Philistines during the Iron IA period. Ceramics were a principal part of that archaeological evaluation. For the settlements in the highlands of Canaan, it is a much more difficult process. The lack of pottery styles that are quantifiably different from known Canaanite types, except for those associated with specific tasks in an agricultural village such as the large collared-rim jars used for storage, place some limitations on identifying particular sites as "Israelite." In addition, the mere presence of cisterns and terraced hillsides becomes a problem when these items have either not been excavated or it has not been determined through other means whether they in fact date to the Iron I period.

For the small villages of the hill country it would have been helpful to have the means to expand their arable plots of land. However, their lack of enough hands to construct and maintain extensive terracing or for that matter the plowing and harvesting of large tracts of land in the valleys between the hills was the principal limitation on their agricultural endeavors. They may well have had the knowledge necessary to cut cisterns in the limestone hillsides to store rainwater near their houses or to construct wine or olive presses to process their grapes and olives (Judg 6:11). Still, these are not technological innovations exclusively associated with the Iron Age. They are present in earlier periods and would have been natural adaptations by the villagers in the hill country.

References to material culture in the narratives found in Joshua and Judges indicate a relatively unsophisticated society occupying the hill country and extending into the Shephelah. They are described as harvesting their fields and bringing the produce to the threshing floor to be processed (Ruth 3:2) and distributed (Num 18:30; Deut 15:14). Many of their weapons, in contrast to their enemies (see Judg 1:19), tend to be household items (woman's millstone—Judg 9:53), herding implements (Shamgar's oxgoad—Judg 3:31), ad hoc objects (Samson's donkey's jawbone—Judg 15:16), or noisemakers (Gideon's trumpets and jars—Judg 7:19). They have village altars, although they are not necessarily devoted to YHWH (Judg 6:28). However, there are also makeshift cultic facilities that simply take advantage of a convenient stone (Judg 6:19–21; 13:19) or a cult corner in a residence (Judg 17:5).

It also is made clear in these episodes, especially those in the Judges account, that the people are only loosely affiliated and are subject to conflict among themselves. For example, Deborah's song (Judg 5:15b–17) castigates the tribes who did not come at her summons to war, and Jephthah had to quell a civil war with the Ephraimites (Judg 12:1–6). Gideon's son Abimelech set himself up as a warlord at Shechem, but quickly had to deal with rivals and was overthrown as the result of his own excesses (Judg 9). And Samson is reminded by the men of the tribe of Judah, who had captured and bound him, that "the Philistines are rulers over us" (Judg 15:11). It is to be expected that in a time of social upheaval and isolated villages spread throughout the hill country that there would be little political cohesiveness. The "Shibboleth" incident (Judg 12:5–6) graphically displays the dialectical variance between these only minimally affiliated groups. However, it is likely that the gross exaggerations of intertribal and external conflicts and violations of basic social civility (gang rape of the Levite's concubine—Judg 19:25–26) have more to do with the argument to establish a monarchy than the social and political reality of the times in the hill country.

Conclusions

Having surveyed what information is available about the invasion of the Sea Peoples and the transformation of the social character of Canaan in the Iron I Age, it is clear that Egypt's hegemony is shattered or badly weakened, that new peoples entered the area and settled themselves along the coast and in the hill country, and that a general reshuffling of ethnic identities took place. Between 1150 and 950 BCE, there is a political vacuum created that allowed for the firm establishment of the Philistines in their five city-states and the Proto-Israelites to grow into a chiefdom that will eventually rival the Philistines for control over much of Canaan. Unfortunately, we lack extrabiblical textual evidence for much of this process and therefore most of what can be said about it is based on archaeological data, which cannot conclusively corroborate the biblical narrative. In fact, much of the biblical account was written and/or edited centuries after the events described and contains a theological and political viewpoint that takes advantage of earlier traditions but is not necessarily concerned with the historical accuracy of its account.

While further archaeological excavations and surveys will be conducted in the future and new evidence may be forthcoming, it is best to remain cautious about sketching out a firm picture of life in Canaan during this time period. As we turn in the next chapter to the development of a monarchy and identifiable Israelite states, this situation does improve with more extra-biblical materials to draw on and Israelite inscriptions that help to add substance to the re-creation of ancient Israel's story during Iron Age II.

4

Transition from Iron I to Iron II

The Early Monarchy

IN THIS CHAPTER THE PRINCIPAL issue to be examined is whether or not a united monarchy existed during the tenth century BCE. That requires an analysis of current archaeological data, extrabiblical records, and the biblical narratives associated with the reigns of Saul, David, and Solomon. In addition, it will be necessary to couple these data with an examination of the social, economic, and political forces that were at work during this period. Since much of these data are still incomplete, it will be difficult to determine conclusively what actually occurred. It is worth noting, however, as has been the case in previous chapters, that the biblical narrative contains a wealth of information that can be tapped. Despite the extensive editing that has taken place over a period of several hundred years, the biblical narrative can help fill in some of the details and can paint a picture of Israel's emergence from a decentralized village culture into a centralized state culture. It is, after all, the story of how these Proto-Israelites eventually were able to compete with their neighbors for political power, for access to trade and natural resources, and for ownership of the land.

EXTRABIBLICAL SOURCES OF INFORMATION

While we do not possess a great deal of verifiable, extrabiblical data on the history of the tenth century BCE, there are several items worth mentioning here. Perhaps most important is the link between David and the city of Jerusalem. Although extensive excavations have taken place over the past century in Jerusalem, constant rebuilding and foundation work reaching down to bedrock has obliterated traces of many of the earlier structures, and erosion has also taken a toll on any artifactual remains. Even so, archaeologists are continuing to identify remains in both Jerusalem and surrounding sites, which they argue are monumental evidence from Iron I. That opinion is not universally held and at this point it is difficult to establish that the city during the tenth century BCE was in fact a large urban center or that it contained the type of monumental architecture usually associated with a capital city. Still, it is important to note that work on Iron I Israel is rapidly developing and continues to be an exciting area of scholarship today.

The state of the question hinges on what has been uncovered of the tenth-century BCE city. These remains include some wall fragments and the "Stepped-Stone Structure," which some believe to have been the architectural underpinning of the biblical Millo mentioned as part of David's fortification of the city (2 Sam 5:9) and later being reinforced by Solomon as the city grew in size (1 Kgs 9:15, 24).[1] To date, all of these architectural remains are located on the ridge south of what is known as the Temple Mount in an area referred to as the City of David.[2] Recently, an additional find on the ridge above and abutting the upper courses of the Stepped Stone Structure, and referred to as the "Large Stone Structure," has been identified by the excavator as a portion of King David's original palace complex.[3] The debate continues on whether it can be substantiated that both of these structures date to Iron I or Iron II, and whether they were actually constructed by the Canaanite/Jebusite inhabitants of Jerusalem in a time period prior to David's reign.[4]

What is important is the current impetus to continue to explore the area in order to see if David made use of these structures after capturing the city, and whether he or Solomon actually construct them. A true capital city requires monumental architecture as a testament to the independence and power of the nation. The choice of Jerusalem as the capital in the tenth century BCE builds on a foundation of authority when it had been one of the political seats of power during the fourteenth-century BCE Amarna period of Egyptian control of Canaan. In addition, it is a location outside the sphere of Philistine control and less susceptible to capture. It also is centrally located without being tied politically to Saul's Gibeah-Gibeon stronghold or to other well-known sites in the Central Hill Country like Bethel or Shechem.

Adding to the picture emerging of the tenth century are the recent excavations at the site of Khirbet Qeiyafa, just to the west of Jerusalem. They have resulted in a great deal of speculation about the city's identity and its possible relation to the early monarchy in Israel. This hilltop fortress in the eastern Shephelah, thirty kilometers southwest of Jerusalem, provides a strategic view of the critical Elah Valley. Archaeological data indicate that it existed during the Iron I and early Iron II periods, a time associated with David's reign (1000–925 BCE). However, efforts to identify the settlement with biblical Shaaraim because of its dual gate system (1 Sam 17:52 and Josh 15:36) or to Elah remain a matter of dispute among scholars, and at this point it may be best to simply note that it was a contemporary settlement with Jerusalem during this period.[5] Its intrinsic importance lies in its geographic placement commanding the route west to Philistia and east to Jerusalem. Furthermore, the recently discovered Proto-Canaanite inscription from this site may be an indication of growing literacy or governmental expansion during this period. That would be an essential element in the development of a bureaucratic state, but at this point the lack of a large body of inscriptions limits the ability to confirm widespread literary or bureaucratic activity.

The ongoing conflict between the Israelites and the Philistines made fortified towns that overlook a buffer zone essential outposts. While some suggest that Khirbet Qeiyafa served as one of David's fortresses, it seems unlikely, given the fact that the site appears to be larger than tenth-century BCE Jerusalem. Qeiyafa's impressive wall system indicates that a great deal of effort went into its construction and there is no indication that David's kingdom or military resources expanded that far to the west. Its location in a disputed borderland area of the Shephelah also makes it possible that the town was politically linked to the geographic zone dominated by the major Philistine city of Gath (Tell es-Safi). However, the artifactual evidence does not indicate a strong Philistine influence or presence. Given that fact, it has recently been suggested the Qeiyafa was either the remnant of or a revival of the Late Bronze Canaanite culture that temporarily (about fifty years) took advantage of the fluid political situation in the Shephelah to establish itself as a rival to both Gath and Jerusalem.[6]

Its destruction toward the end of the tenth century is probably an indication of Gath's growing importance in the region. If that is the case, it would help to explain why such an important and well-fortified site dropped out of the biblical record and was submerged in the collective memory as just an extension of Gath. Furthermore, the suggested links between Qeiyafa and Saul's political territory located north of Jerusalem at Gibeah-Gibeon seem as unlikely as they do to David's Jerusalem.[7] The border area was critical to several political entities and ethnic groups, but Khirbet Qeiyafa may have more to do with Canaanite presence in the area than the fledgling Israelite chiefdoms.

While not dated to the tenth century BCE, the Tel Dan inscription, like the thirteenth-century BCE Merneptah Stele, serves as an extrabiblical trace of the historicity of ancient Israel and in this case of David. It dates to the early eighth century BCE and to the reign of Hazael's successor, the Aramaean king Bar-Hadad III (798–775 BCE). The text is characterized by the typical bombastic style of a victory stele and describes how the ruler of Aram defeated Jehoahaz of Israel and Ahaziah of Judah at the battle of Ramoth-gilead in 798 BCE (2 Kgs 9:1–10:28). What is of particular interest to us at this point is its description of Ahaziah as a representative of the "House of David." In this way evidence is provided of either a dynastic association with David or his successors, or a specific city associated with David and the subsequent rulers of Judah.[8]

We know from other extrabiblical texts that political memory or scribal practice often is tied to the name of the founder of a dynasty. For instance, the name of Omri, the father of King Ahab of Israel (1 Kgs 16:21–30), is mentioned in the annals of the Assyrian kings as the founder of that royal house. Subsequent rulers of Israel, like Jehu, are referred to as a "son of Omri," even though they are unrelated by blood to his house. Thus the Tel Dan reference gives credibility to David as a ruler significant enough that his name is attached to a ruling house. The reference does not, however, prove that a united kingdom, consisting of all of the Israelite tribal territories, actually existed in David's time.

One final example of a significant extrabiblical text is the Bubastite Portal inscription of the 22nd Dynasty, Libyan pharaoh Shoshenq I (conventionally dated to c. 945–926 BCE), found in the Temple of Amun at Karnak. It contains the description of the pharaoh's military expedition into Canaan and includes an extensive list of approximately 150 cities that he claims to have captured or who submitted tribute payments. Because of the wide geographical distribution of these sites, it seems likely that several contingents of Egyptian troops were operating independently in both northern and southern portions of the country. However, and most importantly, the inscription does not list Jerusalem as the focus of any of these expeditionary forces.

For many years, scholars have identified and equated Shoshenq I's campaign with the biblical account of Shishak's invasion of Canaan in the reign of Rehoboam (1 Kgs 14:25–26; 2 Chron 12).[9] Where that equation comes into question is the fact that the biblical account is focused on Jerusalem while Shoshenq's inscription does not mention Jerusalem. Some do say that this omission in the Egyptian version is the result of Rehoboam stripping the gold from Solomon's temple to ransom the city. But that is not entirely satisfying, and as a result some now interpret the biblical narrative as a further attempt by the Deuteronomist to make the case against Rehoboam, citing his failure as a diplomat when dealing with the elders of the northern tribes and his lack of faith in YHWH to protect the capital city.

Additional arguments to separate these two rulers involve both the tactics and the dating of events. The name Shishak is tied in the biblical account to the time of the division of the kingdom, while the Egyptian pharaoh Shoshenq I is generally dated to the mid- to late portion of the tenth century. That would place him closer to the time of Saul and David, and it fits into a period when Egypt maintained regular contacts with Canaan, especially in the Negev where the copper industry and trade continued until the mid-ninth century BCE. Furthermore, if Jerusalem is not a particularly powerful political entity in the late tenth century BCE, it is possible that Shoshenq I is more concerned about curtailing banditry or the political expansion of Saul's Gibeah-Gibeon chiefdom, either of which would have disrupted Egyptian commercial traffic.[10] If that were the case, then Shoshenq's list of towns captured would naturally center on the northern area of Canaan and its major trade routes rather than on Jerusalem. If Shoshenq I and Shishak are indeed the same Egyptian ruler, it seems unlikely that cities in the northern kingdom would be the focus of the campaign. After all, Jeroboam, the first king of the northern kingdom, is described as both a client and an ally of Shishak (1 Kgs 11:40).

Still another suggestion separating the two is that Shoshenq I's reign should actually be pushed down a century to the latter part of the ninth century (between 818 and 808 BCE). That would then mean his strategy was intended to respond to Hazael's Aramaean expansion into northern Canaan. Eliminating that threat would have benefited the Israelite king (possibly Jehoahaz; 2 Kgs 13:4–5), who could then reoccupy cities that had been lost to Aram, and it would explain a pro-Egyptian attitude both by the rulers of the northern kingdom and by the kings of Judah in the early eighth century BCE.[11] What is clear from this example is that inscriptional evidence, unless tied to a fully verifiable context, can lead to various interpretations.

Israelite Historiography

Sorting through the various layers of the biblical narrative that are associated with the establishment of the monarchy and then the reigns of Saul and David is a complex process. To begin with, we have no idea just how much the biblical writers actually knew about their own history. We also have to consider how stories manage to survive intact or are revised over the centuries. Are these tales so central to group identity that they become foundational? Are they so entertaining that they become fixed in social consciousness as integral pieces of the past that the community shares? Or is there enough substance to them that they ring true when recited, at least to the extent that they satisfy those who question or seek answers about Israel's past? The answer may be that history writing or storytelling relies on the best efforts of the writer or storyteller to re-create the past. Like us, they rely on the traces of that past, which are available to them, and quite likely are aware that these traces are not the exact details of the events as they actually happened in the past.[12]

The appearance of dual traditions (see Table 4.1) is one sign of the decisions that are made by the various editors and compilers of oral traditions, whether they are working in the eighth, sixth, or fifth centuries BCE. The result in the received text is a preservation or interspersing of materials rather than the suppression or alteration that is more common in the third-century BCE Septuagint version of the text.[13]

Since the Deuteronomic editors of these materials lived centuries after the events that they describe in their accounts, they may have been forced to resort to authoring a "plausible" rendition of the past for their audience. Collective memory, especially when oral tradition is the primary means of transmission, can be pliable, and therefore the later editors are recording what is current in their own time about early periods.[14] For instance, it is possible that the story of Abimelech's usurpation of power as the warlord of Shechem (Judges 9) is a literary account providing one failed example of how the decentralized groups in Canaan tried to create a more centralized and militarily viable political entity.[15] Similarly, both Saul and David are described as utilizing methods associated with both a warlord and a chief to intimidate (see 1 Sam 11:3–8) or gain influence over the tribal groups (see 1 Sam 30:26).

The editors may well have been exercising a bit of poetic license or theological underpinning in their shaping of the narrative, but it seems likely that there is a limit to what their audience would accept as "historical" or credible. Therefore,

Table 4.1

DUAL TRADITIONS DUPLICATING BIBLICAL ACCOUNTS

Source Parallels in 1 Sam 8–2 Sam 1	*Biblical Citations*
Two depictions of Saul becoming king	1 Sam 9–10:8 and 10:17–27
Two explanations for phrase "Is Saul, to, among the prophets"	1 Sam 10:9–13 and 19:19–24
Saul twice rejected by Samuel	1 Sam 13:1–15 and 1 Sam 15:10–34
Two citations of Samuel's death	1 Sam 25:1 and 1 Sam 28:3
Two stories of David coming to court	1 Sam 16:14–23 and 1 Sam 17:12–58
Two stories of David defeating Goliath	1 Sam 17:19–53 and 1 Sam 21:1–9 (see alternate story in 2 Sam 21:19)
Two occasions when Saul hurls a spear at David	1 Sam 18:10–11 and 1 Sam 19:9–10
Two stories of David leaving Saul's court	1 Sam 19:11–18 and 1 Sam 20
Two incidents when David spares Saul's life	1 Sam 24 and 1 Sam 26
Two versions of David's encounter with Achish, king of Gath	1 Sam 21:11–15 and 1 Sam 27
Two uses by Philistines of the phrase "Saul has killed his thousands, and David his ten thousands"	1 Sam 21:10–11 and 1 Sam 29:1–5
Two descriptions of Saul's death	1 Sam 31 and 2 Sam 1

rather than a strictly fictitious set of stories, the material in these accounts in 1 and 2 Samuel is probably created in large part from what the editors did know based on oral tradition and possibly from extent government records. Admittedly, some portions of the narrative may have conflated the historical-political reality in the tenth and ninth centuries BCE in their description of David's rise. Thus his work as a mercenary chief for Achish of Gath is likely to be a reflection of the fact that Gath is the dominant political force in Philistia and much of the Shephelah until the later ninth century BCE. As a result, the narratives are based on the compilers' re-creation of events. Their efforts are designed so as to avoid imposing an awkward overlay of clearly anachronistic or fantastic details into their storyline.[16]

Among the sources that may have been available to these later editors is a pre-Deuteronomic layer of stories, some of which may have been composed as early as the first half of the ninth century BCE. This material encompasses portions of the stories of the judges and probably includes memories of Samuel, as representative of the premonarchic era. They are portrayed as transitionary figures whose exploits may have contributed to the development of the kingship or to indicate the initial efforts of the Proto-Israelites to evolve beyond the stage of isolated village culture. Interestingly, the tales involving Samuel consist of both pro- and anti-Saul elements in 1 Sam 9–15, at least portions of the so-called apology of David (1 Sam 16–2 Sam 2), and various other pieces that both explain the rationale for the rise of David and also retain some vestiges of Saul's importance when describing the origins of a more complex political arrangement for the tribal groups. In particular, the stories about David's "outlaw" period when he takes on the character of a *habiru* chief (1 Sam 21 and 23) portray him as operating on the political margins between Saul's territory and the important Philistine city of Gath. This material very likely predates the destruction of Gath by the Aramaean king Hazael c. 835 BCE (2 Kgs 12:17).[17]

While we have no way conclusively to prove our surmise, it is possible that these stories, as well as local memories about sites and structures associated with the early monarchy, could have circulated for a very long time and been retained in the collective memory of the people of Judah. In that way the late eighth-century BCE scribal culture that existed in Judah after the destruction of the northern kingdom of Israel could make use of these memories and those contributed by the post-721 BCE refugees from the north when they wrote and rewrote their version of the narratives about their Iron Age past.[18] These refugees from Israel also brought with them a northern perspective on the monarchy as well as stories related to cities and persons (kings and prophets) associated with their region. Pulling together a synthesis of disparate traditions helps to explain why the editors did not fully suppress the multiple traditions about Saul and David, but rather treated them as reliable parallel sources when compiling their history of that era.[19]

Of course, these early compilations of traditions are not the end of the editorial process. Scholars have posited additional overlays of even later editorial work.[20] That includes the editorial refinement of the text that took place in the early sixth century by the Deuteronomistic Historian. When this occurs, the editors have at their disposal earlier segments of tradition and epic, royal annals from both kingdoms, and a knowledge of international events and standardized scribal practices closer to their own time. Their task, which extends into the books of Kings, is to blend together these scraps of data, and occasionally citing sources that for whatever reason they choose not to include in their account (1 Kgs 14:19; 2 Kgs 1:18). In the process they also inject an ideology of an "all Israel" or Pan-Israelite kingdom reaching back to the time of David.

The impetus for the Pan-Israelite concept probably is associated with the efforts of Josiah and his attempt to expand beyond his political base at Jerusalem into what had been the territory of the northern kingdom before the Assyrian conquest in 721 BCE (2 Kgs 23:1–20). In this way, their "spin" on their past history serves the purposes of their principal patrons (Josiah and the temple community in Jerusalem). What better way to justify an expansionist policy than to associate it with the memory of a posited united monarchy under Josiah's ancestor David? At the same time it draws on information that is plausible enough to be accepted as likely events in the original formation of Israel as a nation.[21]

The "all Israel" concept also raises the issue of the exact geographic dimensions of the "kingdoms" of Saul and David. By simply examining the place-names mentioned in the biblical narrative, it seems clear that neither of these leaders held sway over an extensive territory. Saul's center of power, for instance, is located around his hometown of Gibeah and he appears to also have strong ties to the area of Gilead in western Transjordan. When he leads the campaign to liberate Jabesh-gilead in 1 Sam 11:5–11 from the Ammonites, he crosses the Jordan River at Gilgal and travels north and then returns by that route to Gilgal to be proclaimed king by the tribal elders. Furthermore, Saul's son Ishbaal is able to establish himself in Gilead at Mahaniam after his father's death (2 Sam 2:8–9), indicating a continuing association by the household of Saul in that area. Saul and his son Jonathan's military encounters with the Philistines take place within the area of northern Judah and the eastern Shephelah, never in the areas between Bethel and Shechem to the north. Saul's final and fatal battle at Gilboa in the Jezreel Valley (1 Sam 31:1–7) again points to an area accessible through Gilead and indicates the efforts of the Philistines to expand their influence into this important commercial corridor.

In a similar way, the traditions about David indicated his effective area of control prior to becoming king is centered on the area of Hebron and at Ziklag (Tell Sera). He generally operates on the margins of the region controlled by the Philistine city of Gath (Keilah, Adullam, Gob, and the Valley of

Elah). Even as king, his political reach continues to be limited to the territory of Judah and Benjamin, although he does have nominal suzerainty over the northern tribal zone. While he may have been able to call on support from these tribal areas to the north, it seems clear that he never establishes a solid command over that portion of the country. Chiefdoms, like David's, are politically fragile and subject to fragmentation or dissolution if strong leadership is not exercised at all times. For example, Sheba's revolt (2 Sam 20:1–2) points to the ease with which a northern leader could convince the tribes to break from the household of David. Plus, that revolt simply foreshadows the story of the division of the kingdom in Rehoboam's time when the same rallying call goes out to abandon the House of David (2 Sam 20:1b; 1 Kgs 12:16).

POLITICAL TRANSFORMATION IN IRON I

Turning now to the evolving political situation in the Central Hill Country during the settlement period, I refer you back to the discussion in chapter 3 that describes some of the factors that led to the breakdown of Egyptian hegemony over Syria-Palestine during the thirteenth century BCE. To recap, the political and social developments that led to the emergence of Israel as an identifiable national group were facilitated by the weakening of Egyptian administrative control over Syria-Palestine and the elimination of any influence by the Hittites after the invasion of the Sea Peoples around 1200 BCE. The resulting political vacuum allowed new peoples to enter, settle, and prosper in portions of this region of the Levant. To be specific, Egyptian retrenchment facilitated the Philistines' successful investment of the southern coastal region of Canaan during Iron I and contributed to the demographic transformation of the Central Hill Country as new peoples arrived or found refuge there.

During the twelfth and eleventh centuries BCE, the Philistines created a multipolity system consisting of individual city-states, an urban league composed of five cities ruled by their own kings. Despite their lack of political unity, their cooperative arrangement worked well enough for them, at least to the extent that they were able to effectively control or economically exploit a large portion of Canaan.[22] It should be noted, however, that some vestiges of the Late Bronze Canaanite culture did survive in the Shephelah, principally at the city of Beth-shemesh.[23]

And, of course, the Philistines were not the only new settlers in this region. But the question remains: who were these new peoples? Egyptian sources from the late thirteenth to early twelfth century BCE document the appearance of the name Israel as well as Edom and Moab. These references, however, only provide a tenuous link to the appearance of new and identifiable peoples in Syria-Palestine and Transjordan. The archaeological record adds some information on the construction of new settlements, pottery types, and farming methods, but to this point it supplies no inscriptions that name these settlers. Still, using the traces found in the biblical account that described events over the next two centuries, it is plausible that a rivalry developed for political and economic control over Syria-Palestine between the Philistines and these groups of people. Out of this volatile social crucible, ancient Israel eventually emerges.

Thus the factors that assist the Proto-Israelites in their rise are (1) a lack of significant outside interference by either Egypt or Mesopotamia, (2) a restoration of economic activity in areas controlled by the Philistines and in Phoenicia during the twelfth century BCE, and (3) growth in the population of the scattered settlements arrayed in the Central Hill Country. However, the physical restraints placed on hill country settlements by the effects of circumscription and a lack of sufficient arable farm land created an impetus to expand into new territory. In addition, the economic restraints imposed on the Proto-Israelites by the Philistine city-states prevented an expansion of their own trading ventures. And rivalries with other emerging peoples in Transjordan (Edom, Ammon, and Moab) and Aram (Syria) created a situation that demanded greater cooperation among the tribal groups if they were to survive. Otherwise, their settlements either would have had to be abandoned and they would have had to migrate elsewhere (see Judg 18:1b for the Danite resettlement). Alternatively, these peoples might be absorbed culturally and politically into the Philistine sphere, or be culturally eliminated by their stronger neighbors. These factors in turn contribute to an increase in the political struggles during the eleventh century BCE that become the basis of the oral tradition and the setting for the narratives in the books of Judges to 1 Samuel.

TELLING THE STORY OF THE EARLY MONARCHY

Given the paucity of conclusive evidence on the origins of the monarchy in ancient Israel or its early rulers, it is still possible to use elements of political theory to point to why this development eventually did take place (see the summary in 1 Sam 12:6–13). Faced with a life-or-death decision, the first organizational steps begin for the Proto-Israelites with the increasing authority placed in the hands of village elders. Their ability to adjudicate disputes and cooperate with their counterparts in neighboring villages initially facilitated commercial activity and the sharing of innovations in farming techniques, ceramic styles, and political networking. As the population grew and pressure increased to expand their effective territory into areas controlled by the Philistines and other neighboring groups, it is the elders who would be responsible for identifying and empowering local warlords or chiefs, who are charged to deal with a particular crisis within their own area of Canaan.

But for the effectively landlocked Proto-Israelites to escape their spatial trap in the Central Hill Country and to resist the efforts of the Philistines to keep them there, ultimately they find it necessary to shift away from the decentralized political model portrayed in the Book of Judges. They cannot achieve lasting military and economic parity with their rivals when all they can manage is occasional cooperation between villages or clans under the temporary leadership of a warlord (Judg 5:12–18). Lasting success requires a more centralized polity. They must evolve socially and politically, first into an expanded chiefdom model represented by the reigns of Saul and David. Then, once both internal and external factors make it possible, they eventually form a more recognizable, centralized state, possibly under Solomon.

Table 4.2 details the differences found in the biblical text between the settlement period and the emerging monarchic period. While some of these items reflect a more sophisticated analysis of societal needs that developed in later time periods and would not have been initially utilized by the Proto-Israelites, they provide a starting point for examination of the narratives in Samuel to Kings.

Along the way to centralized authority, it is essential to acknowledge the traditions first established in the village culture. For example, the first thing we learn about both Saul and David are their genealogies (1 Sam 9:1–2, 16:1–13).[24] It is essential that these future leaders are rooted in a specific tribe and family that is associated with a particular area of the land. Furthermore, it is also important to describe them as inheritors of their father's authority as a local chief. In that way, it is more palatable for local elders and subsidiary chiefs to accept them and to give them their fealty.[25] Still, it must have been a struggle to do so, given the degree of local authority that the elders must

Table 4.2

COMPARISON BETWEEN SETTLEMENT AND POLITICAL PERIOD

Political Situation in Settlement Period	*Political Transformation—Monarchy*
Local authority by tribal elders with occasional local warlords/judges	Centralization of authority with the consent of tribal elders (1 Sam 11:15; 2 Sam 5:3)
No hereditary transmission of leadership	Hereditary monarchy starts with David (2 Sam 7:4–17)
Lack of cooperation between tribes makes them subject to military and economic threats (Judg 3:13; 4:2; 6:2–6; 15:11)	National leaders/chiefs help unify Israelite military efforts (1 Sam 11:5–11; 14:47–48; 2 Sam 5:17–25; 8:1–14)
No organized efforts to engage in infrastructure projects, trade policy, taxation, or diplomacy	Monumental construction (2 Sam 5:9–12; 1 Kgs 9:15–19); census (2 Sam 24:1); trade (1 Kgs 9:26–28); taxes (1 Kgs 4:22–28); diplomacy (2 Sam 10:1–2; 1 Kgs 5:12)
No bureaucracy or delegation of authority by central government	Nepotism (2 Sam 8:15–18) mixed with appointment of officials (1 Kgs 4:1–19)
YHWH worship not firmly established (Judg 6:25; 17:1–6)	Ark of Covenant brought to Jerusalem (2 Sam 6:1–19); YHWH temple constructed in Jerusalem (1 Kgs 6–8)

surrender. The intellectual and social struggle over these issues can be found in Samuel's warning to the people about the potential abuses of power by kings (1 Sam 8:11–18). Many of his statements are anachronistic, reflecting actual abuses by later rulers, but at their foundation are the political realities associated with setting aside local autonomy in favor of centralized government.

The biblical narratives describe at least some of the steps that the Israelite tribes take in shifting their decentralized multipolity into a more centralized political entity. They feature Samuel, both judge and prophet, who serves as a divine intermediary as well as the emergence of two heroic figures: first Saul and then David. There are occasional links between the activities of the Judges and the success of the later heroes associated with the monarchy. For example, the reference to Samson as the one "who shall begin to deliver Israel from the hand of the Philistines (Judg 13:5b) signals to the later audience the divine intention to raise a leader, who will complete the work that Samson started.[26] Unlike in the stories compiled in Judges 2–16, however, these new-style heroes function as chiefs over larger population groups rather than just as local champions. Their portrayal includes the ability to receive a significant amount of support from the tribal leaders on a regular basis. In addition, the biblical text indicates that they were beginning to take rudimentary steps toward creating the administrative apparatus necessary for the next stage in political development.

By using the material in Table 4.2, it is possible to distinguish how Saul, within his Gibeon-Gibeah domain, and David in Jerusalem differ from the intermittently heroic leaders described in the Book of Judges. For example, none of the judges are able to organize the support of all or even a majority of the tribes to deal with a critical situation, much less determine a long-term, political strategy for all the tribes. In some cases a few of the tribes are able to ally themselves for a temporary period (see the list in Judg 5:12–18), but there is no follow-up or attempt at unification after the military victories. Saul, however, does use his military victory at Jabesh-gilead (1 Sam 11:1–11) as a springboard to recognition of his authority to rule by the tribal leaders (1 Sam 11:12–15). This is not to say that he created a true united monarchy, but he does appear to have established a zone of influence over a period of time. David also solidifies his position as the rightful king first through his successes as one of Saul's military commanders (1 Sam 18:30) and later as a Philistine mercenary (1 Sam 27 and 30), and then through a series of decisive military victories over Israel's enemies (2 Sam 5:17–25, 8:1–14).

The story of Jephthah in Judges 11 is a good model for how this evolving political process works and it serves as a precursor of David's outlaw period (1 Sam 21–30). Jephthah, like the *habiru* bandits described in the fourteenth-century Egyptian El Amarna letters, is expelled from his household in Gilead. He is forced to become the leader of an outlaw gang that preys on caravans and lives a marginal existence. However, when his people need an experienced military chief to rescue them from the Ammonites, they turn to Jephthah and willingly turn over their full allegiance to him as their leader (Judg 11:4–11). In a similar manner, Saul is called on to serve as a war chief to save the besieged city of Jabesh-gilead (1 Sam 11:4–5) and much of his reign is spent in conflict with Israel's enemies. Interestingly, David's early career is almost a mirror image of Jephthah's. He also spends years leading a group of bandits on the margin of Saul's territory (1 Sam 23:1–5). Then, as king he establishes himself in a Jebusite stronghold (Jerusalem; 2 Sam 5:17–25) and also is forced to conduct numerous military campaigns to hold on to his fledgling kingdom.

As long as the tribes remained disorganized and often uncooperative, there was no possibility that they would be able to obtain military or political parity with the Philistines and other neighboring groups. The entire sequence of stories in Judges is predicated on the Israelites being preyed on by stronger peoples and only receiving temporary relief when a local war chief or champion emerges. What makes Saul and David different in this respect is that their narratives include more than one or two battles or confrontations with these foes and there is much more character development in their stories. Saul and David are multidimensional. They deal with not only military crises, but domestic ones as well.

In the judges' tales, the two aborted attempts at passing authority from one generation to another are abject failures (Gideon's son Abimelech—Judg 9–10; Samuel's sons—1 Sam 8:1–3). In fact, it might be said that the judges' inability to establish a multigenerational leadership model is one of the prime arguments for the creation of a monarchy. What muddies this argument is the fact that Saul also fails to pass the throne on to his sons despite the assumption in the text that he plans to do so (1 Sam 20:30–31). Of course, David's rise to power requires the extinction of the Saulide line and therefore, while hereditary monarchy is temporarily derailed, it is firmly reestablished in the succession narrative involving David's sons (2 Sam 13–1 Kgs 2:12). David eventually is succeeded by his son Solomon, although that was not a foregone conclusion (1 Kgs 1:5–14), and it does involve a good deal of political infighting among David's perspective heirs before the dust finally settles.

CHARACTERIZATION OF THE FIRST KINGS

One of the most remarkable aspects of the narrative chronicling the reigns of the first three kings of Israel is how real, how human they seem. They have uncertainties, personal ambitions and strong emotions, failings as leaders, and a desire to pull the tribes together into a more cohesive political unit that can more effectively stand up to environmental crises and military threats. Saul and David in particular are what one would expect of a war chief, who sees the potential for more than what could be accomplished by the judges or local tribal elders.

It is worth noting that despite the primitive political character of their administrations, too heavily dependent on nepotism among their advisers and on marriage alliances to solidify the support of local leaders, they do make strides toward enlarging their sphere of influence and setting precedents for later rulers. It is the shift away from crisis management when David assumes the throne that is the real turning point in the narrative. Even though he will also have to deal with the problems inherent in establishing a hereditary monarchy—chiefly the political ambitions of his sons—there is a sense of being able to imagine the future. Some of that is to be found in the additions or embellishments of the editors, who took storylines and legends about these early rulers and transformed them into a foundation document for their people. And, within just three generations, they created an idealized model, personified in Solomon, as the epitome of efficient kingship. That does not prevent the editors from also using Solomon's great failing, making accommodation for the gods of his many wives, as the basis for the great crisis when the monarchy and the nation divides (1 Kgs 11:31–33). For, after all, they are not just interested in telling a good story. The kings and their new nation are important, but in the end the most important thing to the Deuteronomic editors is how well the people and their leaders adhere to the covenant with YHWH.

To demonstrate how the received narrative is interwoven with the efforts taken to create a central government and to set precedents for later kings to follow, I have mapped out here a series of points to consider. Each of these precedents, while tied to the era of the early monarchy, also is designed to signal how to characterize and preserve the integrity of the monarchy in later periods.

ESTABLISHING POLITICAL PRECEDENTS

1. The "Lord's Anointed"

The political struggles within the houses of Saul and David bring up another point. These very detailed and human dramas are reminiscent of the stories of the ancestors in Genesis. And, like the ancestral narratives, the various episodes embedded in the early monarchic narrative are designed to establish social and legal precedents. Since this is primarily a political narrative, chief among these precedents is legitimacy to rule and the symbols associated with kingship. The anointment ritual in which Samuel, God's prophet and representative, pours olive oil on the head of first Saul (1 Sam 10:1) and then David (1 Sam 16:12–13) transforms them into the "Lord's anointed" ruler. This act is a political gesture. It ties the newly minted king to YHWH as his patron and contains within it a tie to the chief economic asset of the region, the olive. Furthermore, the title and the account of how God's presence entered them (1 Sam 10:2–13; 1 Sam 16:13b), provides them with not only a label or extension to their throne name, but a form of protection against assassination unless that should be God's will. Thus, David is portrayed as regretful for even cutting off "the corner of Saul's robe," a physical representation of the king's authority, and pledges that he would never raise his hand against Saul, "for he is the Lord's anointed" (1 Sam 24:6). Admittedly, this is a self-serving pledge since David has the same title and does not want to set a precedent for the violent overthrow of a ruler. Still, it functions as a check in these narratives and as such would have been employed in later periods, at least in Judah, to serve as a curse on anyone who wished to replace the king through violent means (see David's assertion of its power in 2 Sam 26:9–10).

Perhaps as a reflection of the evolution of the political institutions of the early monarchy, the anointing ceremony assumes a more formal character when Solomon takes his place as king (1 Kgs 1:38–40). As a final act in his career, David provides instructions on how this is to be orchestrated, starting with Solomon riding David's mule as a sign of the transition of power (1 Kgs 1:32–33). Trumpets are to sound to signal his accession, and a cry is to go up demonstrating the people's acknowledgment of his right to the throne (1:34; compare David's entrance into Jerusalem in 2 Sam 6:14–19). The place where the anointing is to take place also plays on tradition and symbolism. It is staged at the spring of Gihon, the principal water source for the city of Jerusalem. Its value will continue to figure in later events in the history of Israel (1 Kgs 20:20; 2 Chron 32:30), and in this case it serves as a reflection of the king's duty to provide life (= water) to the people.

While some of the events in Solomon's investiture ceremony may be a conflation injected by later editors, the taking of a horn of oil from the sacred precincts of the tent of meeting in Jerusalem and his anointing by Zadok, the high priest, in the presence of witnesses (members of his political faction, who will become a part of his court, and his mercenary troops), would be essential to Solomon's claim to the throne over that of his brother and rival Adonijah. The ritual of anointment continues to be a part of royal ceremonies in Judah long after Solomon's time (see Pss 2 and 110). However, in some cases they reflect a restoration of a rightful heir to the throne (Joash in 2 Kgs 11:4–12), or occur in the crisis after the violent death of Josiah and fail to protect the Davidic dynasty from extinction within the next quarter century (2 Kgs 23:30).

Note that there are similar stories that portray how kings of the northern kingdom were chosen by God to become rulers.

However, they are instructed without being anointed to either take a portion of the territory of "David's kingdom" (Jeroboam in 1 Kgs 11:26–38) or, if anointed, are told to violently eliminate the current ruler with no mention of that king being the "Lord's anointed" (Jehu in 2 Kgs 9:1–10). Only Jehu is anointed by a prophet's representative, but that seems more pro forma to the narrative than an essential element.

2. Everlasting Covenant

Intimately tied to the concept of kingship in the reigns of David and Solomon is the everlasting covenant. In essence, this is a promise of divine right to rule for a particular dynasty, starting with David (2 Sam 7:4–17). It appears in the narrative after reference to the failure of Saul's dynasty to perpetuate itself through Michal (6:23), and it adds another layer to the sacrosanct character of kingship associated with the title of Lord's anointed. Interestingly, it also appears in the text as an alternative to David constructing a temple to YHWH in Jerusalem (7:1–3). Later attempts to tie David to the planning, furnishing, and ritual performance in the temple that is constructed in Solomon's reign (1 Chron 28) may be efforts on the part of the postexilic temple community of priests to add greater authority to their institution by tying it back to David. However, for the purposes of setting a political precedent, the everlasting covenant both serves to justify a hereditary line of rulers and provides later Davidic kings a strong argument against regime change. In addition, it is a Deuteronomic counterbalance to the more chaotic political situation recounted about the northern kings, whose dynasties are short-lived and generally ended in violence (see 1 Kgs 15:25–29; 16:8–13).

The covenant God made with Abram/Abraham is a conditional compact. It requires obedience and exclusive worship in order to receive the divine benefits of land and children (Gen

15). In contrast, the everlasting covenant is unconditional. Although David, like Abram, is chosen by God and directed into a new, more prominent role than would have otherwise been possible, the promise to David and to his descendants is that their reign in Jerusalem will extend "forever" (1 Sam 7:12–13, 16). Even though they may commit "iniquity," God will only punish them as needed, but never take back his "steadfast love" (Heb: *ḫesed*) as was the case with Saul (7:14–15). Solomon references the covenant promise made to David in his prayer when the temple is dedicated. He points to his accession to the throne as the natural succession guaranteed by the terms contained in 2 Sam 7:12–16. He dutifully quotes this passage (1 Kgs 8:25) before launching into a series of "if-then" situations (compare Deut 28) that call on God to be magnanimous in granting the necessities of life (rain and protection against enemies). He asks the deity to be just in punishing the people when they fall away from their covenant obligation, and merciful in restoring them to divine favor when they repent (1 Kgs 8:22–53). While much of dedicatory prayer is a later addition by the Deuteronomic editors,[27] it does an excellent job of framing the role of the king and the deity in leading and providing for the needs of the people.

3. Ark of the Covenant

The role of the Ark of the Covenant in the early history of the Israelites is multifaceted. Of course, it serves as a physical reminder of God's presence (possibly a divine footstool; 1 Chron 28:2) and a repository for sacred relics (tablets of the law; Deut 10:2). However, it was also carried into battle (Josh 6), and in so doing it symbolically brings the divine warrior to the battlefield, rallying the courage of the army and striking fear into the hearts of the enemy (2 Sam 4:3–8). In terms of its presence in the Saul-David narrative, there is a clear contrast drawn. Saul makes absolutely no use of the ark despite its previous associations with Joshua (curious since Saul does emulate Joshua by going to Gilgal for his official assumption of power as king; 1 Sam 11:14–15). It is possible that the ark's association with Eli and the shrine at Shiloh (1 Sam 3:3) and its subsequent cloistering at Kiriath-jearim (1 Sam 6:9–7:2) made it an object too dangerous to handle for Saul. Furthermore, Samuel makes no effort to restore the ark to a proper shrine where a priestly community could once again claim ownership and authority.

The question then is why David, in contrast to Saul, felt free to transport the ark from Kiriath-jearim to his new capital at Jerusalem. It may have been a political calculation on his part that the only way to rally the tribes long-term to his kingship is to "capture" or control an object that has a story reaching back to Moses and is associated with Joshua's role in bringing the Proto-Israelites into the land of the covenant. To be sure, the narrative is quick to show that the ark, as a sacred object independent of politics, demonstrates its power during the journey (2 Sam 6:1–11), requiring David to show respect and humility. But, ultimately, the ark becomes the key to David's establishment of Jerusalem as both a political and religious capital for the infant nation.

It is also important to note that this symbol of divine presence never again leaves the city. David's refusal to allow Abiathar and the priests to take it with him when he is forced to go into temporary exile during Absalom's revolt (2 Sam 15:24–25) sets a further precedent that the institution of the kingship and the capital city are both tied to God's presence in Jerusalem. Solomon, too, follows this precedent. After completing the construction of the temple, he transports the ark in ritual procession from the precincts of the city of David to the inner sanctuary of the temple where it is housed, at least until the time of the writers, "to this day" (1 Kgs 8:1–8). Such a careful progression from obscurity to magnificent enclosure for the ark adds further legitimacy to the Davidic dynasty, tying the successive line of kings to divine favor in much the same way as the everlasting covenant. Being placed within a sacred zone, only accessible by the high priest, also prevents the ark from ever again becoming a political asset for a non-Davidic claimant to the throne. And, for Deuteronomic and postexilic editors of this narrative, it solidifies their claims to a temple, with the ark as its heart, where God has chosen to make his name dwell (Deut 12:5–7).

4. Symbols of Power: Monumental Architecture

For the Israelites to emerge from their roots as a village-based culture and take on the trappings of an organized political entity ruled by a king, it is necessary for their ruler to create monumental structures—city walls, temples, and palaces—representative of the power of the state and the people as a whole. The fact that Saul is never credited in the narrative with this important political step is a further argument for David's assumption of power. Of course, both Saul and David spend the bulk of their time engaged in military activities. It is only after the elders throw their support to David after the death of Saul's son Ishbaal (2 Sam 4–5:4), that David turns to architectural pursuits. The initial efforts are practical, including the extension of the Millo to accommodate a larger population in Jerusalem (2 Sam 5:9), but he is quick to turn to the task of constructing a royal residence while he shifted military affairs over to Joab (2 Sam 11:1–2).

This step is critical to the biblical writers, who have as their model the vast palaces and temples in Babylon and the incredible monuments to power in Egypt. It would not do for David's and Solomon's Jerusalem to stand unadorned, even if in reality it is only a small settlement without the grand features of a major city. David is denied the opportunity to construct the temple, probably due to the costs, the distractions of continued military engagements, and political unrest within his household (Absalom's revolt; 2 Sam 15–18) and among the tribes (Sheba's revolt; 2 Sam 20). But it is fair to say that he would have made efforts to extend his authority by constructing hilltop forts along his borders and improving the fortifications of his major settlements.

For the benefit of the Davidic dynasty, however, it is essential that Solomon be depicted in the narrative as a monarch fully in control of his domain and able to dedicate time and resources to improving the infrastructure and defenses of the nation, and building the grand temple to YHWH in Jerusalem (1 Kgs 5–6) and a magnificent palace complex (1 Kgs 7:1–12). Through the use of fine ashlar masonry and the placement of monumental structures in prominent, high places (Zion), the kings also create a contrast between the elites and the common people.[28] Furthermore, both the kings of Israel and YHWH are made to stand out as major entities to be dealt with by other nations.

To be sure, some of what is contained in the text is exaggeration. See for example, the recitation of Solomon's bureaucratic assemblage in 1 Kgs 4:1–19. Any centralized government requires the establishment of administrative offices and the delegation of tasks to regional officials. However, it is unlikely that any of these men had charge of "sixty great cities with walls and bronze bars" (4:13). Similarly, the attribution to Solomon's reign of monumental, six-chambered gates at Hazor, Megiddo, and Gezer (1 Kgs 9:15) seems beyond the scope of his fledgling kingdom. While these gates are more likely to be dated to the ninth century BCE and the northern dynasty of the Omrides,[29] it is understandable that they would have been known to the Deuteronomic editors of this narrative, who wished to create a strong political foundation for the southern kingdom once the northern kingdom was conquered and destroyed by the Assyrians in the eighth century BCE.

THE EARLY MONARCHY: A WORK IN PROGRESS

In the midst of current speculation on the formation of the early monarchy in Israel, it seems appropriate to subtitle this final section "a work in progress." New theories on state formation, archaeological discoveries that assist or redirect our discussion of the scope of David's and Solomon's kingdom, and the possibility that a great deal contained in the Samuel to Kings narrative has been generated during the postexilic Persian period indicate we still have much to learn about the tenth century BCE. Regardless of the historicity of Saul, David, and Solomon, there are some central points that the biblical writers have embedded in their narratives to solidify the institution of the monarchy as it eventually takes shape. The way in which these leaders are portrayed in the text tells us a great deal about how the Israelites, either during the time that they reigned or during the time of the eighth- and sixth-century editors, thought about their rulers. In no case are they shown to be complete paragons of virtue or idealized heroic figures. Instead, they are very human, facing real threats to their people and themselves.

In addition, without extensive archaeological or epigraphic evidence pointing to Jerusalem as a major administrative center during the tenth century BCE, it is better for now to see that period as a focal point for early Israelite organization as they began to emerge as an identifiable political entity. It also is important to understand that the biblical narrative does not reflect a day-by-day or year-by-year account of happenings during the tenth-century BCE Iron I period. For instance, it is not probable that the fledgling political entity led by Saul and later by David was as continuously at war as the narrative seems to suggest. The realities of planting and harvesting, commercial activity, and the inability to mount large military forces and keep them in the field for months at a time would restrict warfare to particular seasons (2 Sam 11:1), and that required periods of rest during which these opponents would carry out normal daily affairs.

Whether they are eponymous founders of the nation or figures collectively formulated by later editors, Saul, David, and Solomon individually and together provide a personified link to the nation's past. Like Moses and Joshua, they are a part of a political genealogy that legitimizes the traditions of the people who became the Israelites. With that said, it would be poor methodology to ignore the stories about these early political figures, for to do so would deprive us of information that contributed to the collective memory of a nation's picture of itself. If nothing else, their efforts are a jumping-off point for the period of the divided monarchy when the experiment in government begun by these early figures comes to its greatest heights and darkest depths.

5

Super-Power Politics in Iron II and the Role of Vassal States

From Jeroboam to Josiah

WHILE THE INTERNATIONAL POLITICAL VACUUM in the Near East during the eleventh to tenth centuries BCE made it possible for new cultures like the Philistines to enter the eastern Levant and new groups like the Proto-Israelites to settle in the Central Hill Country of Canaan, the political strides that these peoples make are curtailed by the end of the ninth century when super powers reemerge in Egypt and Mesopotamia. In the midst of this change in the political winds, this chapter focuses attention on the division of David's and Solomon's kingdom into two separate states: Israel in the north and Judah in the south. The aftermath of that event and the subsequent interaction with both comparable states in Transjordan and international super powers are chronicled both in the biblical narrative and in inscriptional evidence from these political rivals. Archaeological evidence of the Iron II period also provides a great deal more information on settlement patterns, various aspects of state formation, and the development of new technologies that energize the ancient economy.

Some of the uncertainty so evident in previous chapters on the history of ancient Israel is set aside once we transition into the Iron II period. Several things change between 925 and

750 BCE. It is during this time period that the small states, including Israel and Judah, Aram, Ammon, Moab, and Edom, are recognized by and mentioned regularly in the records of the super-power states of Egypt and Mesopotamia. Therefore, instead of working with just a few documents or monumental inscriptions, as has been the case in previous chapters, the history of Israel and Judah between 850 and 586 BCE emerges in a clearer light in the many extrabiblical texts that are now available to us. They provide information on diplomatic, military, and economic interactions between states and give a better sense of the struggle for Israel and Judah to remain independent. Even so, it will still be necessary to sort through the official propaganda contained in the annals, monumental art, and inscriptions produced by the super powers and compare that to the version of events contained in 1 and 2 Kings and some of the prophetic literature in the Bible. By taking all of these data together, a rather stark picture emerges of the inherent difficulties of a small state as it first resists and then is forced to transition into a vassal state under the direct influence of foreign governments. Eventually, the small states become political pawns caught in the middle of international conflicts and intrigues. Ultimately, it is this change from independent, if relatively insignificant states, to vassal states, to conquered and exiled peoples that has a profound effect on the history and culture of the Israelites.

Division of the Kingdom

The death of Solomon and the accession of his son Rehoboam to the throne around 925 BCE occur in a twilight period just before the fortunes of the small states in Syria-Palestine change forever. Despite the political framing that this transition of power receives in the biblical narrative from the Deuteronomic editor (1 Kgs 12:1–19), several things are clear. First, and perhaps foremost, is Rehoboam's journey to Shechem to meet with the tribal elders. If Solomon's kingdom was as firmly established as the text would have us believe, it is incredible that the elders were not summoned to Jerusalem for this summit meeting. In the past, the elders had come to David in his regional center at Hebron when they offered the kingship to him (2 Sam 5:1–3). Since Rehoboam's action reverses this political precedent, his power and the strength of the Household of David are shown to be suspect. It is therefore not a surprise that the fissioning of the nation is the result, following a pattern that had previously been set during Sheba's revolt in David's time (compare 2 Sam 20:1 and 1 Kgs 12:16).

It is clear that this division of the kingdom following the death of Solomon is the decisive factor in transforming a fragile monarchic model into, at least in the northern kingdom, a regional power capable of competing with its neighbors and even expanding its territory. During this same time period, the southern kingdom of Judah remains a secondary state, often subject to the rule or direction of the northern kingdom. Judah's economic impact on the region, given its lack of natural resources and international connections, is also much less than its northern neighbor. Frankly, it is doubtful whether the kings of Judah have the ability to expand their influence beyond the confines of the area encompassed by Hebron, Lachish, and Jerusalem. Thus when we talk about the period of the divided kingdom it is really a tale of the northern kingdom with the southern kingdom operating very much in the shadow of its more powerful neighbor.

These newly minted states begin to distinguish themselves by developing centralized governmental structures: hereditary monarchies, monumental architecture, enhanced infrastructure to facilitate travel and communication, diplomatic relations with other states, an organized military, and a network of experienced bureaucrats tasked with carrying out the instructions and policies of the central government and overseeing public works projects (see 1 Kgs 11:28). This latter group becomes the face of the government in the local area as they regularly enforce official policies, marshal natural resources, collect taxes (generally in the form of grain and olive oil), and draft men into labor and military service.

All of these organizational steps are designed to create a national identity and a measure of separation from other peoples in the region. As long as the Proto-Israelites lived within a decentralized village culture, their boundaries and political vision were limited and there were few differences between themselves and other villages around them. Once the monarchy is established there is a corresponding impetus to create a set of foundational stories such as those found in the ancestral narratives, the exodus event, and the conquest of Canaan. Added to the narrative about the emergence of Israel's first kings, it is possible for the Israelites, whether from the northern or southern kingdom, to formulate a set of collective memories. Then by telling and retelling these stories (Deut 4:1–14) the people gain the ability to recognize themselves as part of a unique political entity. In addition, major cultural boundary markers (covenant with YHWH, circumcision, legal framework) appear as part of the political and religious rhetoric and serve as essential tools in the creation of a national ethos.

Central governments are also distinguished by their volume of paperwork and recordkeeping. For that to happen in Israel and Judah a broader level of literacy than what existed in the tenth century BCE is needed as well as the creation of a professional scribal community to record and carry out government policy. Building on the Proto-Canaanite and Phoenician alphabetic scripts that had begun to be used during the Iron I period, Israelite scribes gradually develop and systematize a distinguishable, Hebrew alphabetic script that facilitates internal and external communication. And, although we have not found a great deal of evidence of this activity since much of it was probably written on parchment or papyrus, it can be assumed that a large body of business and government records is created. A further step in advancing the nation's economy and placing greater control over transactions at all levels is the formulation of standardized weights and measures. Each of these fundamental changes, while still subject to abuse and adulteration by the unscrupulous (Amos 8:5), marks the shift from a decentralized political cooperative into a centralized state with a national rather than a regional perspective.

Framing the Story

Every official record produced by Egyptian or Mesopotamia scribes chronicling the activities and exploits of their kings is shaped to conform to a specific political agenda or national objective. That means that these texts are an overt form of propaganda. Whether they were written on cuneiform tablets or papyrus, inscribed on the walls of a palace or temple, or displayed with artistic representations of battles or other momentous events, their intent is to demonstrate the superiority of their rulers, their military, their gods, and their culture. However, the fact that few beyond the elites in their society could read these accounts suggests that they are designed as a glorification of their ruler's achievements as either a divine personage (pharaohs) or representative of the gods (Assyrian and Babylonian Annals) and a testament to the power of their regime to defeat or dominate any of their rivals.

For example, the description of the pharaoh Thutmose III's siege of Megiddo in 1479 BCE is found inscribed on the walls of the Amun temple at Karnak in the royal residence at Thebes. Portrayed as a monumental figure standing many times taller than his troops or the "feeble" Canaanite forces arrayed against him, the text makes it clear that the pharaoh's confidence in his ability to bring them victory never fails. The Canaanites are shown to be no match for a god-king, who is protected by Amun from harm to his body, and whose arms are reinforced in their power by the god Seth and are quick to smash the forces of the enemy (COS 2:7–13).

While we do not possess similar monumental inscriptions from the time of the Israelite kings, the editors of the Books of Samuel and Kings often borrow their writing style from the Annals of the kings of Egypt and Mesopotamia. For instance, David's liberation of Keilah is accomplished, despite the fear expressed by his men, with the help of YHWH (1 Sam 23:1–5). In a similar manner, after he becomes king, David's early reign is marked in the text by a series of military victories over Israel's enemies, always with "the Lord's help" (2 Sam 8:1–8).

Such success, however, is not always found in the accounts of the kings of the divided kingdom. These narratives are characterized by a heightened level of theological editorializing by both the Deuteronomic editors and the prophets. It is clear that a marked editorial prejudice is present in the Books of Kings primarily aimed at the rulers of the northern kingdom. Very likely it is based on their reaction to the destruction of Israel by the Assyrian empire in 721 BCE, and on the "southern" or Judahite perspective of the Deuteronomistic Historian.

That is not to say that the southern kings are always portrayed as perfect (1 Kgs 15:1–5). However, even when the writers soundly condemn Solomon for his multiple marriages and his tolerance of his wives' foreign gods, their allegiance to the Davidic dynasty never fully wanes. They can describe how an angry YHWH is willing to "tear the kingdom" from Solomon's son (1 Kgs 11:1–13, 33), but then combine this with a citation of God's promise to David of a perpetual ruling dynasty. While Judah may stand alone as the stronghold of the Davidic monarchy after the division of the kingdom, its existence strengthens the argument for the restoration of Davidic rule and the hope that one day all of the tribal territories will be reunited (1 Kgs 11:30–32, 34–36).

REGNAL YEAR SUMMARIES

With the division of the kingdom, the narrative turns to a description of the reigns of each of the kings of Israel and Judah. In their attempt to be comprehensive in their accounting of all of these rulers, the scribes are adhering to models previously developed by Mesopotamian bureaucrats. Thus they employ a conventional structure that forms an obvious pattern as they move from one king to his successor. In each case when the announcement of the accession of a new king occurs, there is generally a reference to the concurrently ruling king in Israel or Judah. Many times the name of the new ruler's mother is also mentioned along with the number of years he reigned. Major accomplishments, or at least those that interest the compiler, are listed, occasionally including an intimate detail such as Asa's diseased feet (1 Kgs 15:23b) or Azariah's leprosy that required him to share government authority with his son Jotham (2 Kgs 15:5). The envelope structure of each entry is then closed with an editorial judgment reckoning whether this king was a "good" or a "bad" king and the location of his tomb.

In some cases, there are mitigating circumstances that suggest that while a particular king of Judah is a worthy successor of David, he did not accomplish everything that the Deuteronomist considered necessary (i.e., did not remove the high places—1 Kgs 15:11–15; 2 Kgs 14:4). There are also frequent references to archival sources from which the editors drew their material (i.e. Annals of the Kings of Israel—1 Kgs 16:20; 2 Kgs 13:12; Book of the Annals of the Kings of Judah—2 Kgs 20:20).

Table 5.1 provides a graphic representation of the reigns of these monarchs until the fall of Samaria ending the monarchy in Israel (721 BCE), and until the destruction of Jerusalem (587–586 BCE) ending the monarchy in Judah. Some of these dates are simply based on the biblical record and are therefore only approximate, while in other cases they are tied to the reigns of specific Assyrian, Babylonian, or Egyptian rulers and are more exact. The uncertainties of assigning specific dates remain a problem and therefore what is presented here should not be

Table 5.1

CHRONOLOGICAL CHART OF THE KINGS OF ISRAEL AND JUDAH

Israel	*Judah*
Jeroboam I (ca. 927–906)	Rehoboam (ca. 926–910)
Nadab (ca. 905–904)	Abijam (ca. 909–907)
Baasha (ca. 903–882)	Asa (ca. 906–878)
Elah (ca. 881–880)	Jehoshaphat (877–853)
Zimri (7 days, ca. 880)	Jehoram (852–841)
Tibni (ca. 880–879)	Ahaziah (840)
Omri (879–869)	Athaliah (839–833)
Ahab (868–854)	Joash/Jehoash (832–803)
Ahaziah (853–852)	Amaziah (802–786)
Joram/Jehoram (851–840)	Azariah/Uzziah (785–760)
Jehu (839–822)	Jotham (759–744)
Jehoahaz (821–805)	Ahaz (743–727)
Joash (804–789)	Hezekiah (727–686)
Jeroboam II (788–748)	Manasseh (698–644)
Zechariah (747—six months)	Amon (643–642)
Shallum (747—one month)	Josiah (642–609)
Menahem (746–737)	Jehoahaz II (609—three months)
Pekahiah (736–735)	Jehoiakim (608–598)
Pekah (734–731)	Jehoiachin (598—three months)
Hoshea (730–722)	Zedekiah (597–586)
Samaria falls 722 BCE	Jerusalem destroyed—586 BCE

considered the final determination of the chronology of the kings of Israel and Judah.[1] Where regnal dates do overlap, that represents either co-regencies when a king and his successor share power or when a usurper claims the throne prior to the death of a king.

JEROBOAM'S ISRAEL

The "party line" of allegiance to the household of David provides the basis for the Deuteronomistic Historian's castigation of the northern kings. To be sure, they may have been aided in their efforts to diminish the accomplishments of these rulers by the constant cycle of short-lived dynasties and their subsequent extinction in the midst of bloody coups led by ambitious military leaders (1 Kgs 15:25–30). However, the extrabiblical records that mention some of the northern kings, in particular Ahab, show that there is much more to the story than the Deuteronomist is willing to tell. But that is the point with propagandists. Working with a specific political agenda, they selectively pick and choose what data to use and what is to be left out of the record.

Thus, when Jeroboam makes his initial appearance in the text, he is given only faint praise with the notation that he is "very able" (1 Kgs 11:28; compare 1 Sam 9:2; 16:12–13). Following an earlier pattern set in the narratives about Saul and David, he is given divine appointment by a prophet when Ahijah relays God's promise that he is to be given charge of ten tribes, but he is not anointed (1 Kgs 11:31). Furthermore, he is cautioned that he must diligently listen to God's commands, walk in God's ways, and keep God's statutes "as David my servant did" (1 Kgs 11:38). The assumption made here is that an idealized version of David's faithful behavior is the standard on which Jeroboam and all future monarchs of Israel will be measured. However, there is no mention of the "forgiveness clause" contained in the everlasting covenant granted to David's household (2 Sam 7:14–16). The offer to Jeroboam is very much a conditional contract predicated on a strict standard of service. The promise of an "enduring house, as I built for David" (1 Kgs 11:38) hinges on absolute obedience without the possibility of redemption should a failure occur. Jeroboam is literally set up to fail.

With that as a foundation, it seems likely that the editors looked back on what they knew of Jeroboam's career and collectively portrayed his efforts in such a way as to create a separate identity for the northern kingdom based on what they termed "Jeroboam's sin." Looked at more dispassionately, it is possible to see that when Jeroboam is proclaimed king by the elders of the northern tribes (1 Kgs 12:20), he is astute enough to recognize what needs to be done to effectively separate the two kingdoms politically. The Deuteronomist couches Jeroboam's actions as the work of a cynical ruler protecting himself from possible rebellion by his people if their loyalties are allowed to remain attached to Jerusalem (1 Kgs 12:26–27).[2] Most of the policies outlined in 1 Kgs 12:26–33, for which he and his successors are condemned (see 1 Kgs 15:34), actually represent practical political choices.

It should be noted that a great deal of the editors' ire against Jeroboam likely is based on his creation of alternative national shrines that diminished the importance of Jerusalem. Excavations at Tel Dan have revealed a large Iron II sacred precinct that contains what appears to be a temple, and the remains of a massive four-horned altar and a large quantity of animal bones suggest this site was used for sacrifice. To date, however, no comparable shrine has been found at the site of Bethel (Tell Beitin).

Table 5.2 details "Jeroboam's sin," pointing out the political value associated with each of his actions and providing an evaluation, based on the Deuteronomic perspective, of why they

Table 5.2

EVALUATION OF "JEROBOAM'S SIN"

Jeroboam's Policy	*Political Value*	*Deuteronomist's Complaint*
Appointed two national shrines at Dan and Bethel at either end of country	People identify with Israelite shrines and do not go to Jerusalem for festivals	Diminishes Jerusalem's temple as the place YHWH makes his name dwell
Placed golden calves in the shrines to represent God's presence	Replaces the ark as the physical symbol of God and creates national pride	Calves are associated with Ba'al worship and violate second commandment (Exod 20:4–6)
Certified the use of local high places for everyday worship	Grassroots support for central government for respecting local worship customs	High places associated with foreign gods and false worship (Num 33:52; 2 Kgs 17:9–11)
Appointed non-Levites to serve as priests at high places and in his two shrines	Ensures political loyalty by appointing these priests and removing Levites' authority	Only Levites can legitimately serve as priests (Num 3:10)
Changed the date of Festival of Booths from the seventh to the eighth month of the calendar	Recognizes the realities of climate and true date of the harvest in northern kingdom	Violates the statute establishing the date of the Festival (Num 29:12)
Set a precedent of the king offering incense on the altar	Added to appointment of priests, king gains authority over temple and priesthood	Only Levitical priests are consecrated to perform altar sacrifices (Num 18:1–7)

are strict violations of divine statutes and an abrogation of the sacred rights of the Levitical priests. Presented in this way, the editors repeatedly refer back to Jeroboam's reign as the basis for the northern kingdom's political and religious problems. Every "bad" king is defined as one who continues the sin of Jeroboam (1 Kgs 16:26; 22:52). Every "good" king, as expected, only appears in the chronicles of the kings of Judah. Each is proclaimed to have done "what was right in the sight of the Lord, as his father David had done" (1 Kgs 15:11; 2 Kgs 18:3).

JEROBOAM: HIS SUCCESSORS AND RIVALRY WITH JUDAH

There is a definite negative tone in the depiction of Jeroboam and his immediate successors, none of whom rise to any great importance. The emphasis in the text is on political intrigue, military coups, and the crimes of these kings that are associated with the sin of Jeroboam. A Deuteronomic motif (the King's Call to Justice) first introduced in the story of David's adultery with Bathsheba (2 Sam 12:1–23), places Jeroboam in a divine courtroom with the prophet Ahijah as his accuser (1 Kgs 14:1–18).[3] The king's multiple "sins" (i.e., political and religious innovations) become the basis for God's death sentence for his household, and provide the justification for the first of many bloody purges after a usurper takes the throne by force (1 Kgs 15:27–30; 16:8–13). The inability of any of these early kings to establish a long-lasting dynasty, while being attributed by the editors to their apostasy, is actually typical of newly established monarchies when there is not a strong tradition of allegiance by the elders and the military to a single ruling household.

That unstable political situation in the north is reversed by the editors in the often very brief biographical notes for the kings of Judah. While Rehoboam and his successors are also far from perfect in the eyes of the Deuteronomist (see the charges against Rehoboam in 1 Kgs 14:22–24), the divine license to eliminate them never appears in the narrative. Furthermore, these southern editors are careful to include a recurring promise of a "lamp in Jerusalem," signifying YHWH's adherence to the promise made to David of a permanent royal regime (1 Kgs 15:4–5; 2 Kgs 8:19).

There are some interesting, if not historically verifiable, details about the strained relations between these two minor states. They are often in conflict (1 Kgs 14:30; 15:16) and occasionally ally themselves with neighboring states such as Aram (1 Kgs 15:18–21). However, there is a sense that the overall political situation in the ninth and eighth centuries BCE is quite volatile in Syria-Palestine, and is similar to the situation described in a Mari text in which a king's official tells his lord that "there is no king who, of himself, is the strongest."[4]

While these petty kings jockey for power and periodically wrench territory away from their fellows, they are easy prey when the international powers once again begin to exercise their imperial ambitions after 850 BCE. And, occasionally, even during the late tenth or early ninth century BCE, a pharaoh of Egypt reaches out to protect economic interests or free travel along the international trade routes in Canaan. That desire to flex their muscles and preserve their economic assets helps to explain the dual-pronged campaign of Sheshonq I (ca. 945–926 BCE) that is discussed in the previous chapter. While it is unlikely that the reference to pharaoh Shishak in Rehoboam's time (1 Kgs 14:25–26) is the same ruler or the same event depicted in the Bubastite Portal inscription at Karnak, it is indicative of how vulnerable the small states were when the larger powers wished to exercise a political or economic agenda in the region.

For about a century, and until they are forced to become unwilling pawns in the international conflicts between Egypt and Assyria, both Israel and Judah as well as Aram and the Transjordanian states of Ammon, Moab, and Edom work to form their own political identity, and they play a chess game for relatively small stakes within their shared region. Eventually, it will be Israel and Aram that will emerge as the dominant players while the others are forced into subservient roles as allies or conquered states. Still, the history of Israel and Judah, as well as the other small states, is marked by brief periods of independence and economic expansion followed by downturns in their fortunes. Some of this fluctuation is based on the competence and/or ambitions of their rulers as well as the relative power of the international powers in Egypt and Mesopotamia.

THE OMRIDE DYNASTY

Some would say that the history—that is, the verifiable history—of Israel begins with Omri around 880 BCE. Jeroboam and his immediate successors are only mentioned in the biblical account and, therefore, like the kings of the early monarchy, are still relegated to tradition rather than history. In contrast, Omri is the first king of the northern kingdom to be mentioned outside the biblical text. His ability to extend Israel's influence is described in the Moabite inscription of King Mesha (835 BCE). This extrabiblical document describes Omri as the oppressor and ruler of Moab "for many days." In addition, the Annals of the Assyrian king Shamaneser III (858–824 BCE) refer to Jehu as the "son of Omri," thus tying him in official court documents to the Omride Dynasty, despite the fact that Jehu is the usurper who brought down the household of Omri (2 Kgs 9–10). That reference is an indication of standard bureaucratic practice in Assyria. Rather than bothering with the details of internal political coups and changes of dynasty in frontier regions, they simply continue to use the name of a king that they have previously attached to that particular country.

Archaeological investigation of the new capital city that Omri built thirty-five miles north of Jerusalem that he named Samaria (1 Kgs 16:24) shows that the site was originally a large agricultural estate with numerous associated installations (vats, storage pits, cisterns). Ceramic remains are consistent with Iron I domestic pottery that is then superseded by Iron II pottery types when the site is transformed into a walled city during the late ninth century BCE.[5] The city is situated on a hill rising 430 meters above sea level and is centrally located in the northern kingdom with command of major travel routes to the north and south. Omri's choice to move the capital slightly west from Tirzah (Tell el-Far'ah North) is consistent with the reasoning David applies when moving his capital from Hebron to Jerusalem. In both cases it breaks with previous political associations (Tirzah is the capital used by Jeroboam and his successors—1 Kgs 15:33). Both cities are more centrally located and are easily defended, and in both cases it facilitates the ruler's desire to make a stronger case for royal authority through the creation of monumental architecture (palace, temple, and massive city walls to defend against sieges) associated with their regime.

Omri's other major accomplishment is the establishment of a household that continues to rule Israel for three generations before succumbing to a military coup led by Jehu (2 Kgs 9). Despite the fact that the biblical narrative only acknowledges Omri as a military commander, who usurps power by killing his rivals and taking the throne, it is clear that he is the model for royal leadership in Israel until its destruction by the Assyrians in 721 BCE. As noted above, even foreign powers grant him notoriety by referring to Israel as "Omri-land" (Sargon II, 721–705 BCE) and referring to later rulers of Israel as a "son of Omri" (Shalmaneser III, 858–824 BCE).

These same Assyrian Annals (Kurkh Monolith) also list Omri's son Ahab as a significant member of the coalition of small states that briefly checks Shalmaneser III's advance into Canaan at the Battle of Qarqar in northern Syria (853 BCE). The Assyrian text lists Ahab's contingent of the alliance forces as two thousand chariots and ten thousand soldiers. That is probably an exaggeration, but its size is an indication by the Assyrian scribes that Ahab is among the most important contributors to the coalition and second only to Hadad-ezer, the ruler of Aram. It is also a testament to the ability, at least temporarily, of these small states to cooperate against a common threat. Unfortunately for them, the Assyrian king continued to campaign into the region throughout his reign and eventually the alliance fell apart and the Assyrians began to absorb them into their empire over the next fifty years.

Given this growing international threat, it is not surprising that the archaeological record during the mid- to late ninth century BCE shows the construction of massive gate systems at Hazor and Megiddo and Gezer, work attributed to Solomon (1 Kgs 9:15), but which are better dated, given the realities of the political situation to the time of the Omrides. Much of the argument that has centered on these gate systems has been based on a dispute over high or low chronologies for the divided monarchy, but until a clearer archaeological picture of the tenth century BCE becomes available, it is best to make attributions based on what we know about a given period rather than try to confirm the biblical account.[6]

As for the biblical record of Ahab's reign, no mention is made of Qarqar or any conflict with the Assyrians during his time. And the only monumental project attributed to Ahab is the reconstruction of Jericho, which cost the architect his two sons (1 Kgs 16:34). In fact, the focus in the Book of Kings is on Ahab's marriage to the Phoenician princess Jezebel and his blatant apostasy in promoting Ba'al worship, which provokes

YHWH's anger against him "more than . . . all the kings of Israel who were before him" (1 Kgs 16:31–33). Such a marriage alliance would have benefited the political and economic position of both parties and Ahab's acceptance of Jezebel's "zeal" in promoting her gods is a parallel to Solomon's practice with his many wives (1 Kgs 11:1–8). Such apostasy, however, was unacceptable to the Deuteronomist and thus it dominates their view of his reign and clouds any positive accomplishments.

Perhaps that is why only regional conflicts are mentioned in the biblical narrative. The account of the nearly continuous rivalry with Aram over territory on their mutual border is highlighted by an encounter with the prophet Micaiah (1 Kgs 22). It also contains an indication of Judah's subsidiary role with King Jehoshaphat coming to Ahab's court and being placed in a position in which he must assist with the upcoming border war. That is further affirmed by the fact that while Jehoshaphat receives a generally positive review by the Deuteronomist (1 Kgs 22:41–50) and the Chronicler (2 Chron 17–19), neither he nor any king of Judah is mentioned in Assyrian texts prior to the end of the eighth century BCE.[7]

The marriage of Ahab's daughter Athaliah to Jehoshaphat's son Jehoram is another indication of political ties between the two kingdoms during this period (2 Kgs 8:25–27). However, the Deuteronomist is quick to condemn the union since she convinces Jehoram "to walk in the way of the kings of Israel" (2 Kgs 8:16–18). It is only when Athaliah is executed in 835 BCE and Jehoram's son Jehoash is restored to the throne that Judah temporarily is able to threw off Omride and Israelite domination (2 Kgs 11:13–20).

Regarding the situation in Moab, we can trace Israel's expansion into the Transjordanian region based not so much on the account of Omri's reign, but on the Moabite inscription of King Mesha dating to the last third of the ninth century BCE. It is necessary, however, to keep in mind that Mesha's statements are royal propaganda designed to raise his status and glorify both his ruling household and their close connection with the Moabite god Chemosh. According to the inscription, Omri took the opportunity to expand his territory eastward into Moab and his successors maintained control for several decades. In so doing, Israel gains control over at least a portion of the Transjordanian Plain north of the Arnon River. Three Moabite cities are mentioned by Mesha in the text: Medeba, Ataroth, and Jahaz. It is unclear, however, whether Omri annexed them to Israel's territory or simply exacted tribute from the large herds of sheep native to that region.

Mesha's rebellion against Israelite control may have been sparked by Ahab's death and the perceived weakness of his successors. In any case, Israel's inability to bring Moab back under its control and the very extensive construction projects described by Mesha are an indication that fortunes are changing for the Omrides. That becomes clear when Jehu, an Israelite military officer, stages a coup that results, according to the biblical account, in the complete elimination of the Omride dynasty (2 Kgs 9–10). There is a certain irony in the fact that Jehu is basically given license to take the throne by the prophet Elisha (2 Kgs 9:1–13). While we have no evidence to corroborate this, it is likely that Jehu's purge of the Omrides, including Queen Jezebel (2 Kgs 9:30–10:28), ended the important alliance with Tyre, something that benefited Hazael and Aram.

Even though Jehu is able to seize power, what we know of him outside the Bible is based on the Black Obelisk inscription of the Assyrian king Shalmaneser III. The text describes the Israelite king bringing tribute (gold, silver, tin, and various luxury items), evidence that he had been forced into or had voluntarily accepted the position of a vassal king within Assyria's zone of political control. It also indicates that the Assyrian ruler has chosen to emphasize the economic value of his campaigning rather than the martial air typical of other

Assyrian kings.[8] The accompanying depiction of this event carved into the stone shows Jehu bowing low to the ground at the Assyrian ruler's feet. Interestingly, Jehu's appearance on this relief is a direct reference to the extent of Assyrian advances in the west. Internal politics or symbolic representation aside, it is clear in this text and its accompanying graphic who represents real power and who is now in a subservient position.

This is not to say that Israel, Judah, or Aram quietly accepted domination by the Assyrians. In fact, it is clear from the Assyrian Annals, the biblical account, and archaeological evidence that over the next century there are numerous rebellions and punitive expeditions by the Assyrians into this region. The most successful leader in Syria-Palestine during the latter half of the ninth century BCE is Hazael of Aram. Some of his exploits appear in Shalmaneser III's campaign accounts. Interestingly, the description of Hazael's seizure of the throne of Damascus ca. 843 BCE, while being "a son of nobody" (ANET, 280), corresponds in general with the story of Elisha's meeting with Hazael and his prophecy that the then military adviser would become the ruler of Aram (2 Kgs 8:7–15).

While he does suffer a defeat at the hand of the Assyrians in 841 BCE (Shalmaneser III's 18th regnal year), Hazael is able to rebuild his forces during the period of political uncertainty just preceding and following Shalmaneser's death in 824 BCE. His efforts were also aided by Egypt's internal problems that prevented them from intervening in Syria-Palestine.[9] In the process Hazael effectively breaks up the anti-Assyrian coalition of small states that had stalled Shalmaneser's advance at Qarqar. He initially creates a sizable territory centered on Damascus. Eventually, he advances north as far as the Euphrates after defeating several other Syrian kings, setting an example for his successors. Thus the inscription of Zakkur, king of Hamath, mentions Hazael's son Bar-Hadad III as the leader of a coalition that continued to threaten his city as his father had before him (COS 2.35, 155).

In the south, Hazael invades both Israel and Judah and conquers and destroys the Philistine city of Gath around 830 BCE (compare 2 Kgs 12:17 and Amos 1:4).[10] Both Judah's king Jehoash (2 Kgs 12:17b–18) and Israel's king Jehoahaz (2 Kgs 13:3–7) found it necessary to either pay Hazael tribute or be decimated in continual clashes with the Syrian forces. The Tel Dan inscription adds further weight to the destructive power of the household of Hazael. Likely recounting the military successes of Bar-Hadad III (796–792 BCE), it celebrates the capture of the city of Dan by the Aramaeans and the death of the kings of both Israel and Judah at his hands (compare the alternative version in 2 Kgs 9:14–28 that ascribes these deaths to Jehu's army).

Given time and greater resources, he might well have threatened Assyria for control of the western Levant. However, restoration of Assyrian military power under Adad-narari III (810–783 BCE) spelled an end to Aram's brief ambitions for dominance in Syria-Palestine. When Damascus falls just around 803 BCE, Israel's chief rival is eliminated and that allows Jeroboam II (789–748 BCE), a loyal vassal of the Assyrians, to restore Israel's control over territory lost to Hazael and his successors. The biblical account of Jeroboam II's expansionist policies (2 Kgs 14:25–27) is probably exaggerated since it includes his control of Hamath on the Orontes River in Syria, an area that is firmly within the Assyrian sphere at this time.[11] Still the account of growing economic prosperity described in the Book of Amos (6:4–8) coupled with archaeological evidence of the presence of more luxury goods during Jeroboam's reign is a further indication that Israel between 800–750 BCE has a freer hand to expand its commercial networks into Transjordan and to the port of Elath, and is not forced continually to defend its borders. It is also during this period that Israel's population grew significantly along with settlement size and attendant authority above the village elder and head of household that had existed in the Iron I period.[12]

Two factors contribute to the end of the period of economic and political independence during the first half of the eighth century. The first is the political chaos that follows Jeroboam II's death. Several of his successors become the victim of violent coups, and some only reign a few weeks or months before succumbing to the ambitions of the next contender for power (2 Kgs 15:8–31). In fact, some of that instability in Israel appears to be the direct result of the growing threat from Assyria and the manipulation of Aram's King Rezin, who favors any claimant who is pro-Aram and anti-Assyria (see Pekah's revolt against Pekahiah in 2 Kgs 15:23–25).

The second and even more decisive factor is the rise of a new king in Assyria, Tiglath-pileser III (744–727 BCE; named Pul in 2 Kgs 15:19). Instead of engaging in the typical seasonal military campaigns designed to plunder or exploit the resources of the small states in Syria-Palestine, this king shifts the Assyrian expansionist strategy and establishes a stable presence in conquered territory. He takes advantage of new advancements in weaponry, a reorganization of the military, and improved logistics to achieve this goal in the nineteen provinces of Hamath in northern Syria. In addition to the usual ideological and territorial basis for campaigning, a further impetus for the change in his policy is based on what Assyria considered an effort on the part of the emerging coalition of small states to cut Assyria off from the lucrative interior trade routes and the Mediterranean seaports.[13]

In addition, combining forces and creating a shared "enterprise zone" that encompasses the coastal highway, the Central Highland trade route, and the King's Highway rather than constantly engaging in petty conflicts, help all of the partners economically. Such an economic block would not be acceptable to the Assyrians, who have no intention of competing with them or relinquishing their ambitions of controlling the economic resources of the western Levant. Thus Tiglath-pileser's expeditions in 734–732 BCE are intended to break up the coalition and gain firm control over Syria-Palestine.

There has been some debate about the purpose behind the formation of the coalition of states that included Israel, Aram, Philistia, and Phoenicia, and whether they were primarily an anti-Assyrian alliance. While it is likely that that is one basis for their cooperation, there is more to the story. For one thing, international events were once again impacting the Levant. Egypt, under the leadership of the Nubian king Piye, is once again making an effort to reunite Upper and Lower Egypt. Piye's Victory Stele that dates to 734 BCE describes his capture of Memphis and the subjugation of his rivals through either military action or treaty (COS 2.42–51). With that accomplished, he was able to reestablish Egypt's coastal link to the trade routes in Philistia and Lebanon and perhaps give the coalition the idea that Assyria might be distracted or even challenged by Egypt (COS 2.42–51).

Sources for the events and the international forces at play during this period include official annals and letters as well as summary inscriptions from Tiglath-pileser's reign and various biblical accounts (2 Kgs 15:29–16:20; Isa 7:1–25; 2 Chron 27:1–28).[14] Thus in Tiglath-pileser's Summary Inscription #7 (ca. 729 BCE) we find a list of vassal rulers, who demonstrated their acknowledgment of Assyria's authority by submitting their tribute payment. For the first time a king of Judah is listed in one of these documents. Ahaz's appearance here provides us with the historical record of Judah's refusal to join the anti-Assyrian coalition (see 2 Kgs 16:7–8). Israel too is and had been for a century a vassal state under the influence of Assyrian hegemony. However, neither Israel nor Aram appear in this tribute list, indicating that their revolt has begun.

Judah's refusal to join the coalition has its roots in weighing the possible consequences of revolt against Assyria as well as a lingering distaste with its condition over most of its history as a subsidiary state to Israel. They had made an effort under King Amaziah (802–786 BCE) to challenge their northern neighbor, but that had ended in a major military defeat and political humiliation (2 Kgs 14:8–14). Furthermore, during the period of Assyrian administrative leadership after 750 BCE, Judah once again loses territory in Gilead to Aram and its new ruler Rezin (see Amos 1:3–5). It is also possible that Rezin assisted the Edomites in taking Elath from Judah's control (2 Kgs 16:6), and he may have incited the Philistines to make trouble on Judah's eastern and southern borders.

Therefore, in the last third of the eighth century BCE, it is not surprising that Judah's King Ahaz seizes an opportunity to step away from the political link to Israel as yet another coalition of small states is formed in the mid-730s. However, when he refuses to join that coalition, Israel and Aram invade Judah with the goal of removing Ahaz from the throne and replacing him with a more amenable ruler of their own choosing (2 Kgs 16:5; Isa 7:1). The biblical account of the Syro-Ephraimitic War notes that Ahaz then asks Tiglath-pileser III for assistance and accompanies his plea with a large tribute payment (2 Kgs 16:7–9). In this way Judah survives much of the conflict to come in the next decade, but at the cost of heavier tribute payments and closer supervision by the Assyrians.

The Assyrian king's Summary Inscriptions #9 and #10 confirm that Tiglath-pileser III uses this opportunity to invade Syria and Israel and puts down their rebellion (COS 2.291). The text describes his taking a massive amount of loot from their cities, and the removal and/or execution of Rezin of Damascus (see 2 Kgs 16:9). In Summary Inscription #4 (COS 2.288), the king recounts how he then places Hoshea on the throne of Israel once their tribute payment is received. This account and the biblical narrative also address Tiglath-pileser's capturing of numerous cities in northern Israel and Gilead and a deportation of a portion of their population (2 Kgs 15:27–29). Probably with Assyrian backing, Hoshea conspires to assassinate king Pekah and thus gain the dubious distinction of becoming Israel's last king (2 Kgs 15:30). Hoshea's ties to the Assyrians are also recorded in the reign of Shalmaneser V (727–722 BCE), as is his subsequent imprisonment for treachery to the Assyrians (2 Kgs 17:1–4).

Clearly, Israel is caught in the thralls of a political spiral from which they cannot escape. It is therefore not surprising that the final move in this game comes when Shalmaneser V and his successor Sargon II (721–705 BCE) react aggressively to Hoshea refusal to pay his annual tribute in 724 BCE and his conspiring with the Egyptians, probably Pharaoh Tefnakhte (2 Kgs 17:4).[15] The massive fortifications that defended Samaria required the Assyrians to stage a three-year siege that eventually resulted in the fall of the starving city in 722 BCE. What follows is the deportation (2 Kgs 17:6) of much of its population in the falling year (Sargon II's Nimrud Prisms—COS 2.295–296). Since they did not destroy the city, Samaria then becomes the seat of Assyrian control in what had been Israel for the next century, and a new population is moved into the area from other regions in the Assyrian empire (2 Kgs 17:24; COS 2.118a: 293). At the same time, Judah and Ahaz benefit from their loyalty to Assyria, regaining some lost territory and escaping the depredations of an invading army.

JUDAH AFTER THE FALL OF ISRAEL

The fall of Israel and the forced deportation of its population is a watershed moment in the history of the Israelites. For one thing it provides the basis for the injection of a very pointed theodicy by the prophets and the Deuteronomistic Historian (see Deut 29:10–28; 2 Kgs 17:7–23; Jer 8:4–12). This ideology overlays historical events, proclaiming that the failure of the Israelites to obey the covenant is the justification for their punishment. In this way what would otherwise be considered the failure of the national deity is set aside, and the argument is made that the only way to prevent the complete extinction of the nation is for the "righteous remnant" to return to full compliance with YHWH and the covenant (see Jer 18:11; Hos 12:2–6; Amos 5:14–15).

Despite the Assyrian deportation, it is likely that the cultural memory embodied in Israel's past history is preserved by the refugees who fled south into Judah. In this way the Elijah-Elisha cycle of stories as well as the prophecies of Hosea survive along with some of the details about the northern kings and the events that took place between the division of the kingdom and the capture of Samaria. Of course, much of that material was revised or reedited by the Deuteronomic Historian to fit into the editors' negative view of the northern kings and their hope for a restoration of the Davidic kingdom.

While it is impossible to fully determine the full extent of northern cultural influence on Judah after 721 BCE, what is clear is that Judah is very aware of their tenuous situation as vassals of the Assyrian kings. Like all of the small nations in Syria- Palestine, they continue to be caught up in the super-power politics as Egypt and Assyria (and later the Neo-Babylonians) jockey for control of this important border area. What is at stake for the major powers is control of the trade routes and Mediterranean ports as well as stores of natural resources, including the cedars of Lebanon, minerals, as well as grain, olive oil, and wine. In addition, during those periods when neither Egypt nor Assyria are able to conquer the other, Syria-Palestine functions as an important buffer area separating the two combatants. Needless to say, the peoples caught in the middle are exploited for their resources and trapped in a combat zone when armies traverse their territory or react to minor revolts.

It is during the period after 721 BCE that Ahaz is succeeded by this son Hezekiah (727–686 BCE) on the throne of Judah, and he initially remains loyal to Assyria. Even though Sargon II's "Great Summary Inscription" (COS 2.118E: 296–297) does record how the Assyrians were forced to put down recurring revolts in the period between 720–710 BCE, Hezekiah is never mentioned as one of the rebels. It is worth noting that at least from the perspective of the prophet Isaiah, Hezekiah's restraint was not a foregone conclusion and required extraordinary measures on the part of the prophet to convince him (Isa 20). Given that Hezekiah heeds the prophet's words, the Assyrian record only mentions Azuri of Ashdod and a usurper named Yamini in Sargon's boastful accounts of sieges, executions of rebels, and the reorganization of Philistine cities under the rule of Assyrian administrators. For the present, Judah remains virtually untouched by events.

A change comes during the window of opportunity presented by a transition of power in Assyria, following the death in battle of Sargon II in 705 BCE. Amid revolts in Babylonia and other parts of the Assyrian empire, the Nubian kings of Egypt and the Babylonian leader Merodach-baladan (Isa 39:1) take the opportunity to tantalize the rulers in Syria-Palestine, including Judah, to consider the possibility of freeing themselves from Assyrian control (see Isa 30:1–5).[16] Hezekiah uses this period of relative freedom from Assyrian scrutiny to initiate a religious reform movement designed to cleanse the worship of YHWH from foreign influences and centralize ritual practice in the Jerusalem temple (2 Kgs 18:4–6; 2 Chron 30–31). Of course, that also means that Hezekiah, with his raids into Philistia and his refusal to submit his annual tribute to the Assyrians (2 Kgs 18:7–8) is asserting himself as David's successor and raises hopes of expanding his rule north into Israel.

Archaeological evidence of Hezekiah's efforts to improve the administrative organization of his nation includes the gathering of agricultural products within his domain into centralized storage facilities at sites like Lachish, and the imposition of *l'mlk* seals on storage jars starting in the last quarter of the eighth century BCE. These seals, incised into the handles of standardized, mass-production storage jars, proclaim that the grain and oil that they contain are the property of the king and the state.[17] In addition, the construction of the Siloam Tunnel, documented by the late eighth-century BCE inscription carved into its wall (COS 2.28: 145), shows his ability to marshal skilled labor to accomplish a remarkable engineering feat whether it was intended to augment Jerusalem's water supply or was part of his long-term preparations for an expected Assyrian reaction to his religious reform and other rebellious acts.

Like so many efforts on the part of the minor kings of Syria-Palestine and despite the Deuteronomist's glowing words about his reign, Hezekiah's window quickly shuts. Sennacherib (704–681 BCE) succeeds Sargon II and quickly moves to suppress the Chaldean revolt in Babylonia that is led by Marduk-apla-iddina II (Merodach-baladan; 2 Kgs 20:12), and he places his own appointee, Bel-ibni, on the throne in Babylon in 703 BCE.[18] With that accomplished, the Assyrian king then returns his attention to the western reaches of his empire. When Sennacherib led a campaign in 701 BCE into Syria-Palestine, many rulers in Phoenicia, including Sidon and Acco, and in Transjordan quickly submitted and sent tribute payments to the Assyrian emperor (RINAP 23.35–54, 192).

However, the rulers of Ashkelon and Ekron in Philistia, and Hezekiah of Judah, chose to resist and they quickly become the target of the invading Assyrian army. Sennacherib first takes Ashkelon and replaces its ruler with one loyal to Assyria. Ekron had deposed their king, Padi, and sent him into the custody of Hezekiah at Jerusalem and allied themselves with the Egyptians. Sennacherib defeats the combined rebel forces at Eltekeh and Tamna, hung the leaders of the anti-Assyrian movement from the walls of Ekron, and restored Padi, whom Hezekiah had quickly released, to his throne (RINAP 23.ii 57–iii 15, 192–193).

It is now Hezekiah's turn to face the displeasure of the Assyrian king. The record of Sennacherib's Third Campaign (RINAP 23.iii 16–42, 193–194) contains a detailed account of an army ravaging the Judean countryside, destroying small towns and gathering large amounts of booty and prisoners (see Micah 1:8–16). While the fate of the city of Lachish, Judah's principal fortress on its western border, is not mentioned in the Assyrian record (see 2 Kgs 18:14), the city's fate is pictured on a bas relief in the palace at Nineveh, showing captives and their few belongings being taken away on foot and in wagons.

Sennacherib's account of the siege of Jerusalem shames Hezekiah as a rebel, who is "overwhelmed by the awesome splendor" of the Assyrian king and is justly bottled up in his capital "like a bird in a cage" (COS 2.119B: 303). There are several biblical passages that record these events and present a variety of perspectives that range from ideological to theological (2 Kgs 18:13–19:37; Isa 36–37; 2 Chron 32:1–22). With that said, what actually happened in 701 BCE at the walls of Jerusalem? Did the Assyrian ambassador, "the Rabshakah," harangue Hezekiah's officials, belittling them for their reliance on Egypt as their ally and throwing in their faces the idea that YHWH had sent the Assyrian horde to punish Hezekiah for removing the high places (Isa 36:4–7)? Is Sennacherib's boastful tone justified when he does not in fact capture Jerusalem and instead accepts a ransom for the city? In other words, it is important to determine the purpose behind how a narrative is written, the ideology of the compilers/scribes/nation, and the story's audience before making any judgment about its potential historicity.[19]

What can be drawn from these various accounts and archaeological evidence is that Judah's cities and towns suffered greatly from the Assyrian invasion. The proffered Egyptian assistance (see 2 Kgs 19:9) mentioned by the Rabshakah does not have a counterpart in the Kushite royal inscriptions from this period.[20] It seems unusual that they are silent on this point, but it may be the hope of the king of Judah rather than the reality of real Egyptian support that is at play in this situation. The Assyrian account, typical of its genre, follows a standard order of events that hinges on whether a ruler or a city (1) submits and presents tribute, (2) rebels and withholds tribute, (3) falls completely and is punished, or (4) ransoms the city and submits to Assyrian rule.[21] Ordinarily, royal ideology also includes a recitation of territory added to the empire, but that is not the case with Sennacherib's Third Campaign.

Leaving a much-diminished Hezekiah in place as king in Jerusalem may have served the emperor's desire to tamp down rebellion in the western reaches of the empire. The extensive list of tribute seems to balance the failure to capture Jerusalem as does the large number of prisoners, some of which are enlisted in the Assyrian army. Furthermore, the biblical account of a second western campaign in which Sennacherib is miraculously defeated seems unlikely (2 Kgs 19:29–37). Sennacherib is assassinated by one or more of his sons in 681 BCE (COS 3.3.95: 244; 2 Kgs 19:37), and his successor Esarhaddon (680–669 BCE) makes no mention of a military defeat at Jerusalem and concentrates his efforts on other priorities such as the rebuilding of Babylon (COS 2.2.120: 306) and campaigning against the Phoenician cities of Sidon and Tyre (ANET, 290–291).[22]

From Manasseh to Josiah and Assyrian Domination

Following Hezekiah's death he is succeeded by his son Manasseh (698–644 BCE), a child of twelve, who may have been hand-picked by the Assyrians or their Judean supporters (2 Kgs 21:1–16). His long reign (fifty-five years) and the venom employed by the Deuteronomist to vilify his many crimes against the covenant with YHWH and his complete submission to Assyrian domination portray Judah receding into the backwaters of international affairs. To be sure, archaeological surveys have revealed that nearly 85 percent of the settlements in the Judean Shephelah were abandoned, probably due to the exile of thousands of these people by Sennacherib.[23] Furthermore, Manasseh is only mentioned in two texts produced by Assyrian scribes in the eighth century BCE. One is a list of vassal rulers, who supplied building materials for Esarhaddon's royal palace in Nineveh (ANET, 291), and the other is a list of kings who were forced to contribute to Ashurbanipal's invasion force against Egypt in 659 BCE (ANET, 294). More recent evaluations of Manasseh's reign, however, suggest that the extended period of peace Judah enjoyed even under strict supervision as a vassal state allowed them to rebuild and even take advantage of the restoration of trade brought on by the increased Assyrian presence.[24]

During the early part of Manasseh's reign, Esarhaddon set his sights on conquering Egypt and punishing Egypt's allies in Phoenicia. That would have required the establishment of Assyrian outposts in Judah and Philistia to supply his army and the presence of these forces would have quieted any calls for rebellion by Judah and the other small states (contra 2 Chron 33:10–17). After an initial defeat in 673 BCE, the Assyrians invade Egypt again two years later and succeed in capturing Memphis and holding control of the Delta while

Pharaoh Taharqa continued to rule Upper Egypt.[25] Assyrian efforts to conquer Egypt continue under Esarhaddon's successor, Ashurbanipal (668–627 BCE). He defeats Taharqa in 667 BCE and drives his army as far south as Thebes (ANET, 294–296). Although this conquest only lasts until 653 BCE, when Psammetichus I restores Egyptian rule, it does give the Assyrians temporary claim to the entire Near East.

While Ashurbanipal still has to deal with revolts in Elam, Phoenicia, Arabia, and by his brother in Babylon, he is able to maintain control of his empire until his death in 627 BCE. Given the strength and long reach of the Assyrians during the seventh century BCE, Manasseh and his court were well advised to remain loyal vassals. Still, the brief reign of Manasseh's son Amon (643–642 BCE; 2 Kgs 21:19–26) that ended in a palace conspiracy and his murder suggests that toward the end of Ashurbanipal's reign there were elements in Judah that hoped to break free from Assyrian rule. In any case, the execution of the assassins and the speedy elevation of Amon's eight-year-old son Josiah by pro-Assyrian members of the court ("people of the land"; 2 Kgs 21:23–24) represent an effort to prevent Assyrian officials from taking notice of internal disputes in Judah.

It is not surprising therefore that the early years of Josiah's reign (642–609 BCE) are not recorded in the biblical account and can be assumed to be a continuation of Manasseh's policies and foreign alliances. The turning point for the biblical writer comes in Josiah's eighteenth year. That date coincides with the period immediately after the death of Ashurbanipal in 627 BCE. Political chaos reigns in the heart of the empire consuming the Assyrian court as Ashurbanipal's heirs fight for the throne, and a Chaldean leader, Nabopolassar, rises in Babylon in 626 BCE and threatens Assyria's control over that important segment of their empire.

As has been the case in the past, the transition of power gives hope at least to the peoples on the fringe of the empire, and vassals like Josiah are able to make some moves toward independence and perhaps even envision a policy of modest expansion of their territory. Confirmation of this possibility is found in the narrative describing the finding of the "Book of the Law" as the temple is being renovated (2 Kgs 22:3–20), and Josiah's subsequent institution of a religious reform like that of his ancestor Hezekiah that centralizes worship in Jerusalem (2 Kgs 23:1–14). There are several possible interpretations of this segment of the biblical text. Some see it as a reflection of the exilic community's focus on Jerusalem as the only true place for the sacrificial cult,[26] while others consider it to be a story created by members of Josiah's court to justify his actions and is later incorporated into the larger Deuteronomic recension of the Book of Kings.[27]

The difficulty in determining exactly how important Josiah or his reform are, however, is based on the lack of extrabiblical references to his reign. It is known that Pharaoh Psammetichus I (664–610 BCE), the founder of the 26th "Saite" Dynasty, gradually moved from being an Assyrian appointed ruler to exercising greater control over the Philistine cities and eventually even Phoenicia as Ashurbanipal became increasingly occupied with the war with Elam.[28] While we have no record of a treaty between Egypt and Judah at this time, it seems reasonable that Josiah would have joined the Philistines in accepting the growing presence of Egypt in Syria-Palestine.

After Ashurbanipal's death in 627 BCE, the major powers begin their maneuvering in an effort to position themselves to take advantage of Assyrian weakness. In particular, the Chaldeans and Medes project themselves as heirs of the Mesopotamian segment of the Assyrian empire while Egypt looks to strengthen its hold on the Levantine coast. It is also possible that these shifts in power give Josiah the opportunity to invade the Assyrian province of Samaria and retake the city of Bethel (2 Kgs 23:15–20), an event celebrated by the

Deuteronomist as the end of Jeroboam's sin when the Bethel shrine and its altar are demolished and even the graves of its priests desecrated (compare 1 Kgs 13:1–3).

More significant than Josiah's excursion is the decision by Psammetichus to oppose the growing power of the Chaldeans and Medes. Seeing that Egypt needed to counterbalance events that were speeding Assyria to its inevitable end, starting in 616 BCE the pharaoh begins strategically to place his forces in the upper reaches of the Euphrates adjacent to their holding in Phoenicia, and to give the Assyrians at least nominal assurances of his support. However, the Babylonian Chronicle records that the Chaldean alliance with the Medes is able to gradually push Assyria's forces back into their hinterland in the upper Tigris region and in 612 BCE the Assyrian capital at Nineveh is captured and utterly destroyed by the allies (ANET, 303–304). All that remains is a final defeat of the remnants of the Assyrian army and the expulsion of the Egyptians from Syria and the coastal areas of Canaan. And that will occur, as noted in the Babylonian Chronicle, in 605 BCE when the crown prince Nebuchadnezzar decisively wins the Battle of Carchemish (BM 21946).[29]

Between the fall of Nineveh and the Battle of Carchemish, Psammetichus I dies and is succeeded by his son Necho II (610–595 BCE). He makes the decision to resume Egyptian intervention in events that had been stalled during the final years of his father. As a result, in the spring of 609 BCE Necho leads an Egyptian army along the traditional coastal route that takes him through the Jezreel Valley at Megiddo and possibly into confrontation with Josiah. The only potential source other than the biblical account (2 Kgs 23:29–30; 2 Chron 35:20–24; compare 1 Kgs 22:29–36) for Josiah's attempt to stop Necho's army at this bottleneck point is a statement by the Greek historian Herodotus (II, 159). However, it more likely refers to a later confrontation between Necho and the new Chaldean king

Nebuchadnezzar II (605–562 BCE) in 601 BCE, which results in a draw and the retreat of Babylonian forces for a couple of years from Syria-Palestine while Egypt captures Gaza.[30] Josiah's death, whether in battle at Megiddo or executed by Necho as a rebel, effectively ends his reform and expansionist policies. Judah relapses into the control of Egypt for the next several years until Nebuchadnezzar is able to challenge once again for control of the area after 605 BCE.

JUDAH'S DEMISE

Josiah's immediate successor, Jehoahaz, is deposed and taken as a hostage by the Egyptians and he is replaced on the throne by his brother Jehoiakim (2 Kgs 23:31–34). Egypt continues to rule over Syria-Palestine until the aftermath of the Battle of Carchemish in 605 BCE when they are forced to withdraw from the area and Nebuchadnezzar begins to establish garrisons there. Interestingly, the Babylonians choose not to remove Jehoiakim from his position as vassal ruler in Judah, but only force him to switch his loyalties. The shift in fortunes that so often characterizes this region then comes into play when Necho's Egyptian forces are able to thwart Nebuchadnezzar's plans to invade Egypt in 601 BCE. Jehoiakim takes the opportunity to renew his allegiance to Egypt and refuses to pay tribute to Babylon (2 Kgs 24:1), and once again Judah becomes the focal point for conflict between the super powers.

The Babylonian record of Nebuchadnezzar's expedition against Jerusalem in his seventh year (598–597 BCE) is very brief, lacking details other than the amount of months it took, his successful capture of "the city of Judah," and his appointment of "a king of his choice," presumably Zedekiah (Wiseman, Chron., 73). His strategy is described in the biblical account, noting the use of auxiliary forces from Moab,

Ammon, and Syria to ravage the land and drive the people into Jerusalem for safety, which seems to be effective (2 Kgs 24:2; Jer 25:9–14). Jerusalem falls in March of 597 BCE. Jehoiachin, who had succeeded his father during the siege, is in turn replaced by his uncle Zedekiah as the vassal king of Judah (ANET, 564; 2 Kgs 24:6–17). As a hostage, Jehoiachin joins a significant number of his people in exile, and one Babylonian text does mention the rations he is given as a ward of the court (ANET, 308; 2 Kgs 25:27–30).

For nearly a decade the situation in Jerusalem remains fairly uneventful under Babylonian authority. The record of Nebuchadnezzar's regnal years that survive indicates that he was occupied by internal intrigues and some minor border skirmishes, and does not lead his army into the west beyond Syria. That does not mean, however, that Zedekiah is an entirely docile vassal. There is an indication that he may have begun negotiations with Edom, Moab, Tyre, and Sidon to test the waters of a potential revolt (Jer 27:1–3). Rather than respond militarily at this point, it seems enough that Nebuchadnezzar had Zedekiah brought to him in Babylon during his fourth year (594 BCE) to reaffirm his oath of loyalty (Jer 51:59).

What changes the political climate and once again raises the hopes of the anti-Babylonian factions in Syria-Palestine in 593 BCE is the success of Psammetichus II in conquering his Nubian rivals in Upper Egypt and his subsequent "grand tour" of Palestine and Phoenicia, which was as much a test of Babylonian control of the area as a way of drumming up allies along the route. Furthermore, in 589 BCE, Psammetichus's successor, Apries, distinguishes himself as an energetic leader and one who might well rival the Babylonians.[31] These prospects for change work to the extent that Zedekiah declares himself in rebellion in 589 BCE by refusing to pay tribute to Babylon, and Nebuchadnezzar uses this provocation to not only deal with an unfaithful vassal but also to signal to Egypt that he still controlled Syria-Palestine (2 Kgs 24:20–25:1).

Setting up his headquarters in Riblah in Syria, Nebuchadnezzar directed a two-pronged attack that sent part of his forces into Lebanon and another column of troops marching south into Palestine. The Lachish Letters provide some insight into the course of this campaign. These ostraca were written as hurried notes on the provisioning of the various Judean watch stations in the Shephelah and efforts to bring Egyptian forces to their aid. For example, Ostraca #3 (COS 3.42B, 79) describes the mission of Konyahu, who has been sent to Egypt to obtain military assistance. And, in fact, Apries does send an expeditionary force that temporarily causes the Babylonians to withdraw from the area of Jerusalem. However, after sending his army in a flanking maneuver to cut off the Egyptians from moving north, Apries in turn withdraws, leaving Zedekiah and Jerusalem to their fate. Lachish ostraca #4 (COS 3.42C, 80) records the desperation of the garrison when they report that the fire signals from Azekah can no longer be seen, and they can only assume that that represents the unstoppable advance of the Babylonian army.

The siege of Jerusalem resumes and after eighteen months the city falls in 587 BCE. After his capture, Zedekiah is brought before Nebuchadnezzar at Riblah and is forced to witness the execution of his sons before being blinded (Jer 39:4–7). The city of Jerusalem is put to the torch and the king's palace and temple of YHWH are completely leveled. Over the following months, a significant number of the people are taken into exile to Babylon (2 Kgs 25:8–21). Archaeological surveys indicate that many of the cities of Judah escaped Jerusalem's fate. Administration of the province is placed in the hands of Gedaliah, a pro-Babylonian member of Zedekiah's court, and he moves the government to Mizpah (2 Kgs 25:22–23) before being assassinated (Jer 41:1). There is no record of how the

Babylonians then govern the province, but presumably they appointed another trained official and provided sufficient military garrisoning to prevent another assassination.

The destruction of Jerusalem in 587–586 BCE and the exile of many of the people of Judah marks a major turning point in the history of Israel and the development of their culture. With the monarchy effectively ended and the sacrificial cult of the Jerusalem Temple put on hold until the exiles return and the temple is rebuilt in 515 BCE, the basic ideology of the people is forced to change. For those who experience the exile period and who choose to retain their identity as Israelites, a new emphasis will emerge that will focus on strict adherence to YHWH-only worship, ritual purity as a mandate for members of the covenant community, and a messianic expectation that promises an end to foreign domination and a restoration of an idealized Davidic monarchy. It is a hard thing to see the pillars of one's life destroyed, but out of the ashes of destroyed Jerusalem, Israel's people and its history live on in a new form.

NOTES

Chapter 1

1. See, for example, Provan, Long, and Longman 2015.
2. Grabbe 2008: 21–35, provides a balanced examination of both viewpoints.
3. Megill 2007: 127–128.
4. See Bosman 2006: 464–465. Note that he compares it to previous scholarly debates in the 1940s and 1950s between those holding the maximalist position and their "revisionist" opponents.
5. Chavalas 1995: 164–165.
6. Miller 2010: 169–170.
7. Machinist 1983.
8. See chapter 2.
9. See the Sumerian King List in ANET: 265.
10. Matthews and Benjamin 2016: 153.
11. See Dever 2001: 53–95, for a description of the development of Syria-Palestinian archaeology.
12. See the discussion of the limitations of Carbon 14 dating in Singer-Avitz 2009: 28, 71.

Chapter 2

1. Faust and Ashkenazy 2009: 36.
2. Greenberg 2003.
3. Cohen 2002: 137.
4. Uziel, Shai, and Cassuto 2014: 303–304.
5. Ilan 2003.
6. See Matthews and Benjamin 2016: 69–70, for the fifteenth-century Annals of Hatshepsut that describe the aftermath of the expulsion of the Hyksos.
7. Na'aman 1994a.
8. Langgut, Finkelstein, and Litt 2013.
9. Egypt is active in Canaan during the 12th Dynasty, the Hyksos period (mid-seventeenth to mid-sixteenth century BCE), as well as after the founding of the 18th Dynasty at the beginning of the New Kingdom c. 1550 BCE. See Bietak 1991: 28 and Morris 2005: 31–32.
10. Davies 2008: 111–112.
11. Pioske 2015b.
12. Matthews 2009.
13. Nienass and Poole 2012: 89.
14. Weeden and Jordan 2012: 143.
15. Zerubavel 1995: 6–7.
16. Schudson 1989: 105.
17. Leahy 1995: 232–233.
18. A *hieros logos*: cult legend; de Vries 2004: 102.
19. Geraty 2015.
20. Assmann 2015: 4.
21. Sparks 2015: 263.
22. Bietak 2015: 20–21.
23. Moshier and Hoffmeier 2015: 106–107.
24. Bietak 2015: 26–29.
25. Propp 2006: 735–762; Redford 2011.
26. Na'aman 2015: 528–529.
27. Halpern 1992: 87–113.
28. Na'aman 2011b: 56–59.
29. Blenkinsopp 2000: 319.
30. Assmann 2015: 11.

31. Additional posited parallels from Egyptian texts are outlined in Sparks 2015: 263–265.

Chapter 3

1. See Dever 1995.
2. Routledge and McGeough 2009: 29.
3. Ben-Dor Evian 2011: 113.
4. James 2015: 246–247.
5. Eriksen 2010: 81.
6. Genz 2013: 477.
7. Collins 2007: 76–77.
8. Singer 1994: 284.
9. Singer 1994: 286–290.
10. Ortiz 2008: 200.
11. Bunimovitz and Lederman 2011.
12. Langgut et al. 2013: 150.
13. Collins 2007: 76–78.
14. Bell 2009: 37–38.
15. Bunimovitz 1994: 199–200.
16. Killebrew 2006: 557.
17. Finkelstein 1996: 231–232.
18. Barako 2013: 41.
19. Yasur-Landau 2010: 287–288.
20. Singer 1993: 296.
21. Yasur-Landau 2012: 194–195.
22. Faust 2015: 176–178.
23. Maeir et al. 2013: 3–15.
24. Faust 2013: 193.
25. Hitchcock and Maeir 2013: 53.
26. Wimmer 2013: 6–8.
27. Eriksen 2010: 5.
28. Yasur-Landau 2010.
29. Ortiz 2008: 200.
30. Yasur-Landau 2010: 280.
31. Maeir 2013: 6.
32. Burdajewicz 1990: 67; Maeir 2013: 14.

33. Maeir 2013: 9.
34. Stockhammer 2012; Maeir 2013: 14–15.
35. Maeir 2013: 10–11.
36. Finkelstein 1988: 130–135.
37. Faust 2013: 206–209.
38. Finkelstein 1994: 171–172.
39. Miller 2005: 16–17.
40. Meyers 2006: 249–250.
41. Dever 1992: 104.
42. Kletter 2002: 39.
43. Langgut et al. 2013: 161.
44. Finkelstein and Langgut 2014: 232.
45. Gibson 2001: 122.
46. Gibson 2001: 137.
47. Hopkins 2007: 152.
48. Finkelstein 1988: 309.
49. Dar 1986: 6.
50. Singer 2013: 25–27.
51. Maeir 2013: 192–193, 240–241.
52. Niemann 2013: 254.
53. Halpern 2001: 290–294.
54. Machinist 2000: 57.
55. Albertz 2007: 356–357.
56. Niemann 2013: 247–248.
57. Niemann 2013: 254–257.
58. McNutt 1999: 75, 238.
59. Eynikel 2011: 50.
60. Rosen 1994: 340.
61. Borowski 1987: 59–62.
62. Hutton 2009: 228–229.
63. van der Toorn 2002: 227–230.
64. Schmitt 2012: 399.
65. Butler 2009: 329.
66. Dutcher-Walls 2014: 106–109.
67. Wilson 2013: 310.
68. Herzog 2007: 21.
69. Na'aman 1994a: 223.
70. Na'aman 2011a: 49–52.

71. Nelson 2002: 47–48.
72. Finkelstein 2011: 106–114; Brooks 2007: 55–56.
73. Brooks 2007: 40–41.
74. Na'aman 2009: 102.
75. Amit 2000: 184–188.
76. Butler 2009: 416.

Chapter 4

1. Killebrew 2003: 340–341.
2. Na'aman 1997: 43.
3. E. Mazar 2006.
4. Faust 2012: 51.
5. Pioske 2015a.
6. Na'aman 2017: 5–6.
7. Finkelstein 2013: 140.
8. Athas 2006: 248.
9. Mayes 2011: 129–130.
10. Finkelstein 2013: 140–141.
11. James and van der Veen 2015: 128–133.
12. Becking 2011: 4.
13. Halpern 2010: 115.
14. Leuchter 2016: 4.
15. Benz 2016: 308–320.
16. Rofé 2016: 447.
17. Finkelstein 2013: 135–136.
18. Pioske 2015a: 91.
19. Halpern 2010: 116–117.
20. See a brief summary in Hoppe 2017: 1–3.
21. Halpern 2010: 121.
22. Benz 2016: 96.
23. Bunimovitz and Lederman 2011.
24. Leuchter 2016: 5.
25. Leuchter 2016: 5–6.
26. Smith 2002: 646–647.
27. Cogan 2001: 292–293.
28. Whitelam 1986: 170.

29. See the discussion of the archaeological debate in Moore and Kelle 2011: 249–255.

Chapter 5

1. See Miller and Hayes 2006: 222–223; Hayes and Hooker 1988; and Galil 1996.
2. Sweeney 2007: 176.
3. Matthews 1991.
4. Munn-Rankin 1956: 74.
5. Tappy 1997: 464–465.
6. Moore and Kelle 2011: 250–257.
7. Kelle 2007: 32.
8. Marcus 1987: 88–89.
9. Kelle 2007: 39.
10. Galil 2007: 80.
11. Cogan and Tadmor 1988: 163.
12. Lemos 2016: 386.
13. Dubovsky 2006: 153–156.
14. See Leuchter and Lamb 2016: 299–301 for a list of these documents.
15. Sweeney 2007: 393.
16. Roberts 2016: 209.
17. Lipschitz 2012: 6–7.
18. Grayson and Novotny 2012: 11–12.
19. Ben Zvi 2003: 89–92.
20. Pope 2014: 117–118.
21. Cogan 2014: 55–57.
22. Cogan 2014: 70–74.
23. Faust 2008.
24. Grabbe 2005.
25. Eph῾al 2005.
26. Nicholson 2012: 366.
27. Na'aman 2011a.
28. Redford 1992: 441–445.
29. Wiseman 1956: 23–25, 67–71.
30. Rainey 2001: 61.
31. Redford 1992: 463–464.

BIBLIOGRAPHY

Albertz, Rainer. "Social History of Ancient Israel." Pages 347–367 in W. G. M. Williamson, ed., *Understanding the History of Ancient Israel*. Oxford: Oxford University Press, 2007.

Amit, Yairah. *Hidden Polemics in Biblical Narrative*. Leiden; Boston: Brill, 2000.

Assmann, Jan. "Exodus and Memory." Pages 3–15 in Thomas Levy et al., eds., *Israel's Exodus in Transdisciplinary Perspective: Text, Archaeology, Culture, and Geoscience*. New York: Springer, 2015.

Athas, George. "Setting the Record Straight: What Are We Making of the Tel Dan Inscription?" *Journal of Semitic Studies* 51 (2006): 242–255.

Barako, Tristan J. "Philistines and Egyptians in Southern Coastal Canaan during the Early Iron Age." Pages 37–51 in Ann E. Killebrew and Gunnar Lehmann, eds., *The Philistines and other "Sea Peoples" in Text and Archaeology*. Atlanta: SBL, 2013.

Becking, Bob. "David between Ideology and Evidence." Pages 1–30 in Bob Becking and Lester L. Grabbe, eds., *Between Evidence and Ideology*. Boston: Brill, 2011.

Bell, Carol. "Continuity and Change: The Divergent Destines of Late Bronze Age Ports in Syria and Lebanon across the LBA/Iron Age Transition." Pages 30–38 in Christoph Bachhuber and R. Gareth

Roberts, eds., *Forces of Transformation: The End of the Bronze Age in the Mediterranean*. Oxford: Oxbow Books, 2009.

Ben-Dor Evian, Shirly. "Egypt and the Levant in the Iron Age I–IIA: The Pottery Evidence." *Tel Aviv* 38 (2011): 94–119.

Benz, Brendon C. *The Land before the Kingdom of Israel: A History of the Southern Levant and the People Who Populated It*. Winona Lake, IN: Eisenbrauns, 2016.

Ben Zvi, Ehud. "Malleability and Its Limits: Sennacherib's Campaign against Judah as a Case-Study." Pages 73–105 in Lester L. Grabbe, ed., *"Like a Bird in a Cage": The Invasion of Sennacherib in 701 BCE*. JSOTSup 363; Sheffield: Sheffield Academic Press, 2003.

Bietak, Manfred. "Egypt and Canaan during the Middle Bronze Age." *Bulletin of the American Schools of Oriental Research* 281 (1991): 27–72.

Bietak, Manfred. "On the Historicity of the Exodus: What Egyptology Today Can Contribute to Assessing the Biblical Account of the Sojourn in Egypt." Pages 17–37 in Thomas Levy et al., eds., *Israel's Exodus in Transdisciplinary Perspective: Text, Archaeology, Culture, and Geoscience*. New York: Springer, 2015.

Blenkinsopp, Joseph. *Isaiah 1–39: A New Translation with Introduction and Commentary*. New York, NY: Doubleday, 2000.

Borowski, Oded. *Agriculture in Iron Age Israel*. Winona Lake, IN: Eisenbrauns, 1987.

Bosman, Hendrik. "Three Rounds with a Heavyweight in the 'Maximalist-Minimalist Contest': A Review of the Dever Trilogy." *Scriptura* 93 (2006): 457–466.

Brooks, Simcha S. "From Gibeon to Gibeah: High Place of the Kingdom." Pages 40–59 in John Day, ed., *Temple and Worship in Biblical Israel*. New York: T & T Clark, 2007.

Bunimovitz, Shlomo. "Socio-Political Transformations in the Central Hill Country in the Late Bronze-Iron I Transition." Pages 179–202 in Israel Finkelstein and Nadav Na'aman, eds., *From Nomadism to Monarchy: Archaeological and Historical Aspects of Early Israel*. Jerusalem: Israel Exploration Society, 1994.

Bunimovitz, Shlomo, and Zvi Lederman. "Canaanite Resistance: The Philistines and Beth-Shemesh—a Case Study from Iron Age I." *Bulletin of the American Schools of Oriental Research* 364 (2011): 37–51.

Burdajewicz, M. *The Aegean Sea Peoples and Religious Architecture in the Eastern Mediterranean at the Close of the Late Bronze Age.* Oxford: BAR Int. Ser. 558, 1990.

Butler, Trent. *Judges.* Nashville, TN: Thomas Nelson, 2009.

Chavalas, Mark W. "Recent Trends in the Study of Israelite Historiography." *JETS* 38 (1995): 161–169.

Cogan, Mordechai. *1 Kings.* AB 10. New York: Doubleday, 2001.

Cogan, Mordechai. "Cross-examining the Assyrian Witnesses to Sennacherib's Third Campaign: Assessing the Limits of Historical Reconstruction." Pages 51–74 in Isaac Kalimi and Seth Richardson, eds., *Sennacherib at the Gates of Jerusalem: Story, History and Historiography.* Boston: Brill, 2014.

Cogan, Mordechai, and Hayim Tadmor. *II Kings.* AB 11. New York: Doubleday, 1988.

Cohen, Susan. *Canaanites, Chronologies, and Connections: The Relationship of Middle Bronze IIA Canaan to Middle Kingdom Egypt.* Winona Lake, IN: Eisenbrauns, 2002.

Collins, Billie Jean. *The Hittites and Their World.* Atlanta, GA: Society of Biblical Literature, 2007.

Dar, Shimon. *Landscape and Pattern: An Archaeological Survey of Samaria, 800 BCE–636 CE.* Oxford: BAR, 1986.

Davies, Philip R. *Memories of Ancient Israel: An Introduction to Biblical History—Ancient and Modern.* Louisville, KY: Westminster/John Knox, 2008.

Dever, William G. "The Late Bronze-Early Iron I Horizon in Syria-Palestine: Egyptians, Canaanites, 'Sea Peoples,' and Proto-Israelites." Pages 99–110 in William Ward and Martha Joukowsky, eds., *The Crisis Years: The 12th Century BC: From beyond the Danube to the Tigris.* Dubuque, IA: Kendall/Hunt, 1992.

Dever, William G. "Ceramics, Ethnicity, and the Question of Israel's Origins." *Biblical Archaeologist* 58/4 (1995): 200–213.

Dever, William G. *What Did the Writers Know and When Did They Know It? What Archaeology Can Tell Us about the Reality of Ancient Israel.* Grand Rapids, MI: Eerdmans, 2001.

de Vries, Simon J. "Human Sacrifice in the Old Testament in Ritual and Warfare." Pages 99–121 in J. Harold Ellens, ed., *The Destructive Power of Religion: Violence in Judaism, Christianity, and Islam*, vol. 1. Westport, CT: Praeger, 2004.

Dubovsky, Peter. "Tiglath-pileser III's Campaign in 734–732 B.C.: Historical Background of Isa 7; 2 Kgs 15–16 and 2 Chr 27–28." *Biblica* 82 (2006): 153–170.

Dutcher-Walls, Patricia. *Reading the Historical Books: A Student's Guide to Engaging the Biblical Text.* Grand Rapids, MI: Baker Academic, 2014.

Eph'al, Israel. "Esarhaddon, Egypt, and Shubria: Politics and Propaganda." *Journal of Cuneiform Studies* 57 (2005): 99–111.

Eriksen, Thomas H. *Ethnicity and Nationalism*, 3rd ed. New York: Palgrave Macmillan, 2010.

Eynikel, Erik. "'Now There Was No Smith to Be Found throughout all the Land of Israel' (1 Sam 13:19)—A Philistine Monopoly on Metallurgy in Iron Age I?" Pages 41–50 in Hermann M. Niemann and Matthias Augustin, eds., *"My Spirit at Rest in the North Country (Zechariah 6.8).* Frankfurt am Main: Peter Lang, 2011.

Faust, Avraham. "Settlement and Demography in Seventh-Century Judah and the Extent and Intensity of Sennacherib's Campaign." *Palestine Exploration Quarterly* 140 (2008): 168–194.

Faust, Avraham. "Did Eilat Mazar Find David's Palace?" *Biblical Archaeology Review* 38/5 (2012): 47–52, 70.

Faust, Avraham. "The Shephelah in the Iron Age: A New Look on the Settlement of Judah." *Palestine Exploration Quarterly* 145 (2013): 203–219.

Faust, Avraham. "Pottery and Society in Iron Age Philistia: Feasting, Identity, Economy, and Gender." *Bulletin of the American Schools of Oriental Research* 373 (2015): 167–198.

Faust, Avraham, and Yosef Ashkenazy. "Settlement Fluctuations and Environmental Changes in Israel's Coastal Plain during the Early Bronze Age." *Levant* 41 (2009): 19–39.

Finkelstein, Israel. *Archaeology of the Israelite Settlement.* Jerusalem: Israel Exploration Society, 1988.

Finkelstein, Israel. "The Emergence of Israel: A Phase in the Cyclic History of Canaan in the Third and Second Millennium B.C.E." Pages 150–178 in I. Finkelstein and N. Na'aman, eds., *From Nomadism to Monarchy: Archaeological and Historical Aspects of Early Israel.* Jerusalem: Israel Exploration Society, 1994.

Finkelstein, Israel. "The Philistine Countryside." *IEJ* 46 (1996): 225–242.

Finkelstein, Israel. "Tell el-Ful Revisited: The Assyrian and Hellenistic Periods (with a New Identification)." *Palestine Exploration Quarterly* 143 (2011): 106–118.

Finkelstein, Israel. "Geographical and Historical Realities behind the Earliest Layer in the David Story." *Scandinavian Journal of the Old Testament* 27 (2013): 131–150.

Finkelstein, Israel, and Dafna Langgut, "Dry Climate in the Middle Bronze I and its Impact on Settlement Patterns in the Levant and Beyond: New Pollen Evidence." *Journal of Near Eastern Studies* 73/2 (2014): 219–234.

Galil, Gershon. *The Chronology of the Kings of Israel and Judah.* New York: Brill, 1996.

Galil, Gershon. "David and Hazael: War, Peace, Stones and Memory." *Palestine Exploration Quarterly* 139 (2007): 79–84.

Genz, Hernann. "'No Land Could Stand before Their Arms, from Hatti . . . on . . .'? New Light on the End of the Hittite Empire and the Early Iron Age in Central Anatolia." Pages 469–477 in Ann E. Killebrew and Gunnar Lehmann, eds., *The Philistines and Other "Sea Peoples" in Text and Archaeology.* Atlanta: SBL, 2013.

Geraty, Lawrence. "Exodus Dates and Theories." Pages 55–64 in Thomas Levy et al., eds., *Israel's Exodus in Transdisciplinary Perspective: Text, Archaeology, Culture, and Geoscience.* New York: Springer, 2015.

Gibson, Shimon. "Agricultural Terraces and Settlement Expansion in the Highlands of Early Iron Age Palestine: Is There Any Correlation between the Two?" Pages 113–146 in Amihai Mazar, ed., *Studies in the Archaeology of the Iron Age in Israel and Jordan.* JSOT Supp. 331. Sheffield: Sheffield Academic Press, 2001.

Grabbe, Lester L. "The Kingdom of Judah from Sennacherib's Invasion to the Fall of Jerusalem: If We Only Had the Bible . . ." Pages 78–122 in Lester L. Grabbe, ed., *Good Kings and Bad Kings.* New York: T & T Clark, 2005.

Grabbe, Lester L. *Ancient Israel: What Do We Know and How Do We Know It?* New York: T & T Clark, 2008.

Grayson, A. Kirk, and Jamie Novotny. *The Royal Inscriptions of Sennacherib, King of Assyria (704–681 BC), Part 1.* Winona Lake, IN: Eisenbrauns, 2012.

Greenberg, Raphael. "Early Bronze Age Megiddo and Bet Shean: Discontinuous Settlement in Sociopolitical Context." *Journal of Mediterranean Archaeology* 16 (2003): 17–32.

Halpern, Baruch. "The Exodus from Egypt: Myth or Reality?" Pages 86–117 in Hershel Shanks et al., eds., *Rise of Ancient Israel*. Washington, DC: Biblical Archaeology Society, 1992.

Halpern, Baruch. *David's Secret Demons: Messiah, Murderer, Traitor, King*. Grand Rapids, MI: Eerdmans, 2001.

Halpern, Baruch. "The Historiography of Samuel." Pages 113–122 in A. Graeme Auld and Erik Eynikel, eds., *For and against David: Story and History in the Books of Samuel*. Leuven: Peeters, 2010.

Hayes, John H., and Paul K. Hooker. *A New Chronology for the Kings of Israel and Judah and Its Implications for Biblical History and Literature*. Atlanta: John Knox, 1988.

Herzog, Ze'ev. "State Formation and the Iron Age I–Iron Age IIA Transition: Remarks on the Faust-Finkelstein Debate." *Near Eastern Archaeology* 70 (2007): 20–25.

Hitchcock, Louise, and Aren Maeir. "Beyond Creolization and Hybridity: Entangled and Transcultural Identities in Philistia." *Archaeological Review from Cambridge* 28 (2013): 51–73.

Hopkins, David. "'All Sorts of Field Work': Agricultural Labor in Ancient Palestine." Pages 149–172 in Norman K. Gottwald and Robert Coote, eds., *To Break Every Yoke: Essays in Honor of Marvin L. Chaney*. Sheffield: Sheffield Phoenix Press, 2007.

Hoppe, Leslie J. "The Strategy of the Deuteronomistic History: A Proposal." *Catholic Biblical Quarterly* 79 (2017): 1–19.

Hutton, Jeremy M. "The Levitical Diaspora (I): A Sociological Comparison with Morocco's Ahansal." Pages 223–234 in J. David Schloen, ed., *Exploring the Long Durée: Essays in Honor of Lawrence E. Stager*. Winona Lake, IN: Eisenbrauns, 2009.

Ilan, David. "The Middle Bronze Period (circa 2000–1500 B.C.E.)." Pages 331–342 in Suzanne Richard, ed., *Near Eastern Archaeology: a Reader*. Winona Lake, IN: Eisenbrauns, 2003.

James, Peter. "Kings of Jerusalem at the Late Bronze to Iron Age Transition—Forerunners or Doubles of David and Solomon?" Pages 236–257 in Peter James and Peter G. van der Veen, eds., *Solomon and Shishak: Current Perspectives from Archaeology, Epigraphy, History, and Chronology*. Oxford: Achaeopress, 2015.

James, Peter, and Peter G. van der Veen. "When Did Shoshenq I Campaign in Palestine?" Pages 127–136 in Peter James and Peter G. van der Veen, eds., *Solomon and Shishak: Current Perspectives from Archaeology, Epigraphy, History and Chronology*. Oxford: Archaeopress, 2015.

Kelle, Brad E. *Ancient Israel at War, 853–586 BC*. Essential Histories 67. Oxford: Osprey, 2007.

Killebrew, Ann E. "Biblical Jerusalem: An Archaeological Assessment." Pages 329–345 in Andrew G. Vaughn and Ann E. Killebrew, eds., *Jerusalem in Bible and Archaeology: The First Temple Period*. Atlanta: SBL, 2003.

Killebrew, Ann E. "The Emergence of Ancient Israel: The Social Boundaries of a 'Mixed Multitude' in Canaan." Pages 555–572 in Aren Maeir and Pierre de Miroschedji, eds., *"I Will Speak the Riddles of Ancient Times": Archaeological and Historical Studies in Honor of Amihai Mazar*. Winona Lake, IN: Eisenbrauns, 2006.

Kletter, Raz. "People without Burials? The Lack of Iron I Burials in the Central Highlands of Palestine." *Israel Exploration Journal* 52 (2002): 28–48.

Langgut, Dafna, Israel Finkelstein, and Thomas Litt. "Climate and the Late Bronze Collapse: New Evidence from the Southern Levant." *Tel Aviv* 40 (2013): 149–175.

Leahy, Anthony. "Ethnic Diversity in Ancient Egypt." Pages 225–234 in Jack Sasson, ed., *Civilizations of the Ancient Near East*. Peabody, MA: Hendrickson, 1995.

Lemos, T. M. "Kinship, Community, and Society." Pages 379–395 in Susan Niditch, ed., *The Wiley Blackwell Companion to Ancient Israel*. Chichester, UK: John Wiley and Sons, 2016.

Leuchter, Mark. "The Rhetoric of Convention: The Foundational Saul Narratives (1 Samuel 9–11) Reconsidered." *Journal of Religious History* 40 (2016): 3–19.

Leuchter, Mark A., and David T. Lamb. *The Historical Writings: Introducing Israel's Historical Literature*. Minneapolis, MN: Fortress, 2016.

Lipschitz, Oded. "Archaeological Facts, Historical Speculations and the Date of the LMLK Storage Jars: A Rejoinder to David Ussishkin." *Journal of Hebrew Studies* 12 (2012): 1–15 in http://www.jhsonline.org.

Machinist, Peter B. “Assyria and Its Image in First Isaiah.” *Journal of the American Oriental Society* 103 (1983): 719–787.

Machinist, Peter B. “Biblical Traditions: The Philistines and Israelite History.” Pages 53–69 in Eliezer Oren, ed., *The Sea Peoples and Their World: A Reassessment*. Philadelphia: University Museum, 2000.

Maeir, Aren M. “Philistia Transforming: Fresh Evidence from Tell eṣ-Ṣafi/Gath on the Transformational Trajectory of the Philistine Culture.” Pages 191–242 in Ann E. Killebrew and Gunnar Lehmann, eds., *The Philistines and Other “Sea Peoples” in Text and Archaeology*. Atlanta: SBL, 2013.

Maeir, Aren M., L. A. Hitchock, and L. K. Horwitz. “The Construction and Transformation of Philistine Identity.” *Oxford Journal of Archaeology* 32 (2013): 1–38.

Marcus, Michelle I. “Geography as an Organizing Principle in the Imperial Art of Shalmaneser III.” *Iraq* 49 (1987): 77–90.

Matthews, Victor H. “The King’s Call to Justice.” *Biblische Zeitschrift* 35 (1991): 204–216.

Matthews, Victor H. “Back to Bethel: Geographical Reiteration in Biblical Narrative.” *JBL* 128 (2009): 151–167.

Matthews, Victor H. “Remembering Egypt.” Pages 419–427 in Thomas Levy et al., eds., *Israel’s Exodus in Transdisciplinary Perspective: Text, Archaeology, Culture, and Geoscience*. New York: Springer, 2015.

Matthews, Victor H., and Don C. Benjamin. *Old Testament Parallels: Stories and Laws from the Ancient Near East*, 4th ed. Mahwah, NJ: Paulist, 2016.

Mayes, Andrew D. H. “Pharaoh Shishak’s Invasion of Palestine and the Exodus from Egypt.” Pages 129–144 in Bob Becking and Lester L. Grabbe, eds., *Between Evidence and Ideology*. Leiden: Brill, 2011.

Mazar, Eilat. “Did I Find King David’s Palace?” *Biblical Archaeology Review* 32/1 (2006): 16–27, 70.

McNutt, Paula. *Reconstructing the Society of Ancient Israel*. Louisville, KY: Westminster/John Knox, 1999.

Megill, Allan. *Historical Knowledge, Historical Error*. Chicago: University of Chicago Press, 2007.

Meyers, Carol. “Hierarchy or Heterarchy? Archaeology and the Theorizing of Israelite Society.” Pages 245–254 in Seymour Gitin et al., eds., *Confronting the Past: Archaeological and Historical Essays on Ancient Israel in Honor of William G. Dever.* Winona Lake, IN: Eisenbrauns, 2006.

Miller, J. Maxwell, and John H. Hayes. *A History of Ancient Israel and Judah*, 2nd ed. Louisville, KY: Westminster/John Knox 2006.

Miller, Robert D., II. *Chieftains of the Highland Clans: A History of Israel in the 12th and 11th Centuries* B.C. Grand Rapids, MI: Eerdmans, 2005.

Miller, Robert D., II. "A 'New Cultural History' of Early Israel." Pages 167–198 in Lester L. Grabbe, ed., *Israel in Transition: From Late Bronze II to Iron IIA (c. 1250–850 BCE): Volume 2.* New York: T & T Clark, 2010.

Moore, Megan B., and Brad E. Kelle. *Biblical History and Israel's Past: The Changing Study of the Bible and History.* Grand Rapids, MI: Eerdmans, 2011.

Morris, Ellen F. *The Architecture of Imperialism: Military Bases and the Evolution of Foreign Policy in Egypt's New Kingdom.* Leiden: Brill, 2005.

Moshier, Stephen O., and James K. Hoffmeier. "Which Way Out of Egypt? Physical Geography Related to the Exodus Itinerary." Pages 101–108 in Thomas Levy et al., eds., *Israel's Exodus in Transdisciplinary Perspective: Text, Archaeology, Culture, and Geoscience.* New York: Springer, 2015.

Munn-Rankin, J. M. "Diplomacy in Western Asia in the Early Second Millennium B.C." *Iraq* 18 (1956): 68–110.

Na'aman, Nadav. "The 'Conquest of Canaan' in the Book of Joshua and in History." Pages 218–281 in Israel Finkelstein and Nadav Na'aman, eds., *From Nomadism to Monarchy: Archaeological and Historical Aspects of Early Israel.* Jerusalem: Israel Exploration Society, 1994a.

Na'aman, Nadav. "The Hurrians and the End of the Middle Bronze Age in Palestine." *Levant* 26 (1994b): 175–187.

Na'aman, Nadav. "Cow Town or Royal Capital? Evidence for Iron Age Jerusalem." *Biblical Archaeology Review* 23/4 (1997): 43–47, 67.

Na'aman, Nadav. "The Sanctuary of the Gibeonites Revisited." *Journal of Ancient Near Eastern Religion* 9 (2009): 101–124.

Na'aman, Nadav. "The 'Discovered Book' and the Legitimation of Josiah's Reform." *Journal of Biblical Literature* 130 (2011a): 47–62.

Na'aman, Nadav. "The Exodus Story: Between Historical Memory and Historiographical Composition." *Journal of Ancient Near Eastern Religions* 11 (2011b): 39–69.

Na'aman, Nadav. "Out of Egypt or Out of Canaan? The Exodus Story between Memory and Historical Reality." Pages 527–533 in Thomas Levy et al., eds., *Israel's Exodus in Transdisciplinary Perspective: Text, Archaeology, Culture, and Geoscience*. New York: Springer, 2015.

Na'aman, Nadav. "Was Khirbet Qeiyafa a Judahite City? The Case against It." *Journal of Hebrew Scriptures* 17 (2017): 1–40 in http://purl.org/jhs

Nelson, Richard D. *Deuteronomy*. Louisville, KY: Westminster/John Knox, 2002.

Nicholson, Ernest W. "Once Again Josiah and the Priests of the High Places (II Reg 23.8a.9)." *Zeitschrift für die alttestamentliche Wissenschaft* 124 (2012): 356–368.

Niemann, Hermann M. "Neighbors and Foes, Rival and Kin: Philistines, Shepheleans, Judeans between Geography and Economy, History and Theology." Pages 243–264 in Ann E. Killebrew and Gunnar Lehmann, eds., *The Philistines and Other "Sea Peoples" in Text and Archaeology*. Atlanta: SBL, 2013.

Nienass, Benjamin, and Ross Poole. "The Limits of Memory." *International Social Science Journal* 62 (2012): 89–102.

Ortiz, Steven M. "Recent Trends in Philistine Archaeology and Biblical Studies." Pages 191–204 in Richard S. Hess et al., eds., *Critical Issues in Early Israelite History*. Winona Lake, IN: Eisenbrauns, 2008.

Pioske, Daniel. "Memory and Materiality: The Case of the Early Iron Age Khirbet Qeiyafa and Jerusalem." *Zeitschrift für die alttestamentliche Wissenschaft* 127 (2015a): 78–95.

Pioske, Daniel. "Retracing a Remembered Past: Methodological Remarks on Memory, History, and the Hebrew Bible." *Biblical Interpretation* 23 (2015b): 291–315.

Pope, Jeremy. "Beyond the Broken Reed: Kushite Intervention and the Limits of *l'histoire Événementielle*." Pages 105–160 in Isaac Kalimi and Seth Richardson, eds., *Sennacherib at the Gates of Jerusalem: Story, History and Historiography*. Boston: Brill, 2014.

Pritchard, James B. *Ancient Near Eastern Texts Relating to the Old Testament, 3rd ed.* Princeton, NJ: Princeton University Press, 1969.

Propp, William H. C. *Exodus 19–40. A New Translation with Introduction and Commentary.* New York: Doubleday, 2006.

Provan, Iain, Victor P. Long, and Tremper Longman III. *A Biblical History of Israel*, 2nd ed. Louisville, KY: Westminster John Knox, 2015.

Rainey, Anson. "Herodotus's Description of the East Mediterranean Coast." *Bulletin of the American Schools of Oriental Research* 321 (2001): 57–63.

Redford, Donald B. *Egypt, Canaan, and Israel in Ancient Times.* Princeton, NJ: Princeton University Press, 1992.

Redford, Donald B. "Some Observations on the Traditions Surrounding 'Israel in Egypt.'" Pages 279–364 in Oded Lipschits et al., eds. *Judah and the Judeans in the Achaemenid Period. Negotiating Identity in an International Context.* Winona Lake, IN: Eisenbrauns, 2011.

Roberts, J. J. M. "The Divided Monarchy." Pages 197–212 in Susan Niditch, ed., *The Wiley Blackwell Companion to Ancient Israel.* Chichester, UK: John Wiley and Sons, 2016.

Rofé, Alexander. "Properties of Biblical Historiography and Historical Thought." *Vetus Testamentum* 66 (2016): 433–455.

Rosen, Baruch. "Subsistance Economy in Iron Age I." Pages 339–351 in Israel Finkelstein and Nadav Na'aman, eds., *From Nomadism to Monarchy: Archaeological and Historical Aspects of Early Israel.* Jerusalem: Israel Exploration Society, 1994.

Routledge, Bruce, and Kevin McGeough. "Just What Collapsed? A Network Perspective on 'Palatial' and 'Private' Trade at Ugarit." Pages 22–29 in Christoph Bachhuber and R. Gareth Roberts, eds., *Forces of Transformation: The End of the Bronze Age in the Mediterranean.* Oxford: Oxbow Books, 2009.

Schmitt, Rüdiger. "Rites of Family and Household Religion." Pages 387–428 in Rainer Albertz and Rüdiger Schmitt, eds., *Family and Household Religion in Ancient Israel and the Levant.* Winona Lake, IN: Eisenbrauns, 2012.

Schudson, Michael. "The Present in the Past versus the Past in the Present." *Communication* 11 (1989): 105–113.

Singer, Itamar. "The Political Organization of Philistia in Iron Age I." Pages 132–141 in A. Biran and J. Aviram, eds., *Biblical Archaeology Today, 1990*. Jerusalem: Israel Exploration Society, 1993.

Singer, Itamar. "Egyptians, Canaanites, and Philistines in the Period of the Emergence of Israel." Pages 282–338 in Israel Finkelstein and Nadav Na'aman, eds., *From Nomadism to Monarchy: Archaeological and Historical Aspects of Early Israel*. Jerusalem: Israel Exploration Society, 1994.

Singer, Itamar. "The Philistines in the Bible: A Short Rejoinder to a New Perspective." Pages 19–27 in Ann E. Killebrew and Gunnar Lehmann, eds., *The Philistines and Other "Sea Peoples" in Text and Archaeology*. Atlanta: SBL, 2013.

Singer-Avitz, Lily. "Carbon 14—The Solution to Dating David and Solomon?" *Biblical Archaeology Review* 35/3 (2009): 28, 71.

Smith, Mark S. "Remembering God: Collective Memory in Israelite Religion." *Catholic Biblical Quarterly* 64 (2002): 631–651.

Sparks, Brad C. "Egyptian Texts Relating to the Exodus: Discussions of Exodus Parallels in the Egyptology Literature." Pages 259–281 in Thomas Levy et al., eds., *Israel's Exodus in Transdisciplinary Perspective: Text, Archaeology, Culture, and Geoscience*. New York: Springer, 2015.

Stockhammer, P. W. "The Change of Pottery's Social Meaning at the End of the Bronze Age: New Evidence from Tiryns." Pages 164–169 in C. Bachhuber and R. G. Roberts, eds., *Forces of Transformation: The End of the Bronze Age in the Mediterranean: Proceedings of an International Symposium Held at St. John's College, University of Oxford, 25–26th March 2006*. Oxford, 2009.

Stockhammer, P. W. "Conceptualizing Cultural Hybridization in Archaeology." Pages 43–58 in P. W. Stockhammer, ed., *Conceptualizing Cultural Hybridization: A Transdisciplinary Approach*. Berlin; Heidelberg: Springer-Verlag, 2012.

Sweeney, Marvin A. *I & II Kings: A Commentary*. Louisville, KY: Westminster/John Knox, 2007.

Tappy, Ron. "Samaria." Pages 463–467 in Eric M. Meyers, ed., *The Oxford Encyclopedia of Archaeology in the Near East*, vol. 4. New York: Oxford University Press, 1997.

Uziel, Joe, Shai Itzhaq, and Deborah Cassuto. "The Ups and Downs of Settlement Patterns: Why Sites Fluctuate." Pages 295–308 in

John Spencer et al., eds. *Material Culture Matters: Essays on the Archaeology of the Southern Levant in Honor of Seymour Gitin.* Winona Lake, IN: Eisenbrauns, 2014.

van der Toorn, Karel. "Recent Trends in the Study of Israelite Religion." Pages 223–243 in Gerard Wiegers, ed., *Modern Societies and the Science of Religion: Studies in Honour of Lammert Leertouwer.* Leiden: Brill, 2002.

Weeden, Chris, and Glenn Jordan. "Collective Memory: Theory and Politics." *Social Semiotics* 22 (2012): 143–153.

Whitelam, Keith W. "The Symbols of Power: Aspects of Royal Propaganda in the United Monarchy." *Biblical Archaeologist* 49 (1986): 166–173.

Wilson, Ian D. "Conquest and Form: Narrativity in Joshua 5–11 and Historical Discourse in Ancient Judah." *Harvard Theological Review* 106 (2013): 309–329.

Wimmer, Andreas. *Ethnic Boundary Making: Institutions, Power, Networks.* Oxford: Oxford University Press, 2013.

Wiseman, D. J. *The Chronicles of Chaldaean Kings (626–556 B.C.) in the British Museum.* London: British Museum Publications, 1956.

Yasur-Landau, Assaf. *The Philistines and Aegean Migration at the End of the Late Bronze Age.* Cambridge: Cambridge University Press, 2010.

Yasur-Landau, Assaf. "The Role of the Canaanite Population in the Aegean Migration to the Southern Levant in the Late Second Millennium BCE." Pages 191–197 in Joseph Maran and Philipp W. Stockhammer, eds., *Materiality and Social Practice: Transformative Capacities of Intercultural Encounters.* Oxford: Oxbow Books, 2012.

Zerubavel, Yael. *Recovered Roots: Collective Memory and the Making of Israeli National Tradition.* Chicago: University of Chicago Press, 1995.

Zwickel, Wolfgang, and Pieter van der Veen. "The Earliest Reference to Israel and Its Possible Archaeological and Historical Background." *Vetus Testamentum* 66 (2016): 1–12.

SCRIPTURE INDEX

SUBJECT INDEX

www.ingramcontent.com/pod-product-compliance
Ingram Content Group UK Ltd.
Pitfield, Milton Keynes, MK11 3LW, UK
UKHW041845200726
13854UKWH00005BA/2175